Illustrators:
Larry Bauer
Kathy Bruce

Editors:
Maria Seghers
Mary Kaye Taggart

Editorial Project Manager:
Karen J. Goldfluss, M.S. Ed.

Editor-in-Chief:
Sharon Coan, M.S. Ed.

Art Director:
Elayne Roberts

Cover Artists:
Sue Fullam
Keith Vasconcelles

Imaging:
David Bennett
Alfred Lau

Product Manager:
Phil Garcia

Publishers:
Rachelle Cracchiolo, M.S. Ed.
Mary Dupuy Smith, M.S. Ed.

Cooperative Learning Activities
for
MATH
PRIMARY

Authors:

Grace Jasmine
Julia Jasmine, M.A.

Teacher Created Materials, Inc.
P.O. Box 1040
Huntington Beach, CA 92647
ISBN-1-55734-656-9

Table of Contents

Introduction

Welcome to the wonderful world of cooperative learning. This book is designed to help primary students learn math skills while actively engaged in cooperative activities based on widely accepted general strands of mathematical thought.

A Complete Resource Book

This book provides everything you need to present math concepts using cooperative learning activities. It includes not only innovative ideas but also practical suggestions and blackline masters to help you put the ideas into action in your classroom.

The first sections explain how to make cooperative learning a part of your curriculum. They include an overview, instructions, and activities for introducing cooperative learning to your students and parents, guidelines for setting up groups, ideas for a special activity center, and suggestions for assessment and portfolios.

The rest of the book provides a wide range of cooperative activities separated into these strands:

- **Attributes and Classification**—sorting by characteristics
- **Games and Rules**—developing mathematics of language and logic
- **Understanding Numbers and Numeration**—developing number sense by doing activities with numbers
- **Understanding Arithmetic Operations**—working with the concepts
- **Visualizing and Representing Shapes**—developing spatial sense
- **Dealing with Data**—organizing and representing information
- **Location and Mapping**—estimating and measuring distances; writing directions
- **Process of Measurement**—exploring and comparing
- **Measuring Geometric Figures**—becoming familiar with a variety of shapes; using non-standard units of measure
- **Exchange**—trading equivalent shapes; comparing money values

You may focus on the units that are relevant for your classroom or use them in sequential order.

Easy to Use

This book is designed with the busy teacher in mind. Each activity unit contains a lesson plan which explains the **purpose** of the unit, the **skills** to be taught, and the **materials** that are needed, all of which will fit into one "math tub." A rectangular plastic dishpan would be a perfect "math tub" for each group. This **Math in a Tub** bonus feature will be fully explained in the following pages.

The **procedures** for teaching the unit are described in detail. Ways **to simplify** the unit are provided. These suggestions allow you to adapt the activity to the pre-cooperative learners in a classroom or to shorten the activity to fit into a tight schedule. Ways **to expand** the unit are also provided to challenge advanced students and to continue a lesson that needs further development in the classroom.

A **teacher script** is provided to make framing the activity simple and motivating. It is designed to be an aid in addressing the beginning learner. You may choose to use it as is or to modify it to fit your own teaching style.

Each lesson plan includes suggestions for **evaluation and processing**.

Overview

Cooperative Learning Activities for Math was designed to help the busy teacher combine math concepts and cooperative learning easily into the regular classroom curriculum. For primary children, the mastery of cooperative learning is just beginning, so any attempt at implementing the cooperative learning process should be streamlined and easy to prepare so that it may be carried out successfully. The format of *Cooperative Learning Activities for Math* is designed to fill this need.

It's Really This Easy!

Each cooperative activity in this book is designed to fit into a tub (like a rectangular plastic dishpan). Everything you need can be assembled and placed conveniently in one easily transportable container for each math group. All you have to do is prepare the tubs and, at the beginning of your activity, distribute one tub with all the materials needed for the activity to each group. (See "Materials" section of the teacher pages for a listing of the items you will need. In addition, a "Math in a Tub Layout" page is provided at the end of each lesson. It serves as a visual representation of the materials that the groups will need.) This way you can be free to facilitate the activity, which is such a vital part of the cooperative process.

The Math Club

We have designed this book to revolve around an easy-to-use center. The center for all of these activities is called The Math Club. Your math club center will be a place to store all of your needed materials, a place to conduct whole-class and large group demonstrations and activities, a place to meet before and after the activity to discuss what happened, and possibly a place to watch and listen to math-related audio visual materials. It is also an attractive, colorful addition to your classroom that students will enjoy showing to parents at Open House.

It's Nice to Be Organized

Each activity is organized the same way, using the same construct to make your work easier and allow you to get to the enjoyable part—actual involvement in your students' learning experience. Each activity has the following pages included in this book: an activity page which describes the activity in its entirety, a math tub layout page giving a picture of what your math tubs will look like for this activity/investigation, and group and individual worksheets to be used by the students at the completion of each group activity. Additional teaching pages provide additional ideas, instructions, or information needed to facilitate the activity effectively. Some activities have reproducible patterns to make your job easier.

The Fun in Discovery

We hope that using this book will generate enthusiasm about math from a very early age, as well as give your students some practical logic skills and the structure for some very important thinking skills. The easy format will give you more opportunities to make your classroom exciting and relevant, and the learning process more enjoyable for everyone.

Overview *(cont.)*

Beginning the Book

To begin cooperative learning on a successful note, focus on the whole-class activities on pages 6–10. In this way, students can begin to interact as a whole class, and then in pairs in a positive, non-threatening manner.

These activities will help you to build an attitude of friendliness and cooperation in your classroom before attempting to organize student groups. Additionally, whole-class and pair activities will provide you with opportunities for assessing individuals to best determine members for each group. (See "Selecting Cooperative Groups," pages 11–15.)

Cooperative Learning Groups

This book has been written for a classroom with 30 students, or six groups of five. Simply add or subtract groups, or students in a group, to best serve your class's particular needs. Remember, in cooperative learning, it is best to use an *uneven* number of students in each group whenever possible.

What About Results?

One of the best reasons for introducing cooperative learning throughout the curriculum is that children benefit from them in distinctly observable ways. After completing the activities in this book, look for student improvement and mastery in the following areas:

> - Cognitive and high-order learning skills
> - Communication and conflict-resolution skills
> - Oral language skills
> - Written language skills
> - Self-esteem
> - Ability to work cooperatively with others
> - Understanding of math concepts

How Else Can This Book Be Used?

In addition to its usefulness with the beginning learner, this book has many possibilities for use with ESL students. In addition to the emphasis on basic concepts, the simplified, interest-intensive activities will help with motivation for language acquisition.

Whole-Classroom Readiness and Activities

Easing into Cooperative Learning

Prepare your students for cooperative learning by conducting whole-class cooperative activities. Whole-class activities are especially conducive to creating a comfortable, safe environment in which students have some knowledge and understanding of one another. It is helpful to ease into the cooperative experience since many beginning students have never had the experience of cooperative interaction.

Parallel Players and Pre-Cooperative Learners

The younger the children are, the less comfortable they will feel in group situations. Most toddlers and preschoolers parallel play. This means that they play near each other at separate tasks. To begin the transition from parallel play to pre-cooperative learning, teachers can focus on teaching children how to get along within the classroom setting. Page 7 offers many activities that support this.

Alphabetical Name Game

Secret Secret

Shoe Hunt / Partner Hunt

Concepts such as sharing and taking turns are understood by the pre-cooperative learner, and while a pre-cooperative learner may not always feel comfortable trying to share or take turns, these are ideas he or she will recognize. Remember, becoming a cooperative learner is a process. Many adults have yet to master the idea in their work situations. Be aware of your students. When they have had enough of a cooperative activity, turn to a less stressful and more autonomous one.

Partner Play

Cooperation is an important component in any classroom. When children cooperate, they have the opportunity to think about and assimilate new ideas.

Use the whole-class activities on page 9 to nurture the cooperative atmosphere within your classroom. Each activity is followed by suggested partner play. To help ease your children into the concept of cooperative learning, allow them at first to work with one partner only.

Picture Journal

Rest and Remember

You may wish to have your students become very comfortable with partner play before beginning the cooperative activities in the rest of the book, or you may find it beneficial to use both group and partner activities, depending on your students' learning needs.

Whole-Classroom Readiness and Activities *(cont.)*

1. **Shoe Hunt/Partner Hunt:** Students can use the pattern on page 8 to color two matching shoes. They will write their names on the provided lines. Half the students can then put one "shoe" into a box, bowl, or other container and leave the second shoe on their desks. The other half will take turns picking a shoe and matching it to the one on the owner's desk. The student whose shoe was picked will then become that student's partner. Each set of partners will talk together to find out three things about one another. They can write what they have learned on the shoes. Use the completed shoes for a bulletin board display.

   This activity is a good icebreaker for shy children or those who do not know each other. Used at the beginning of the school year, it will set the stage for building cooperative teams based on friendly interaction.

2. **Secret Secret:** Choose a leader to begin. Have students stand in a circle. The first person tells the second person a secret. It is then repeated until it reaches the end of the circle and is said aloud. Have the person who began the secret and the person who heard it last compare the differences in the secret. This activity will help students to understand the importance of listening carefully in their cooperative groups.

3. **Walking Through the Neighborhood, I Saw a…:** This is a whole-class participation alphabet game. Students stand or sit in a circle. Choose someone to lead with the sentence-starter, "I was walking through the neighborhood, and I saw a…" He or she fills in the blank with something that starts with the letter "A." The next person in the group must think of something that begins with the letter "B," and so on with the rest of the alphabet. (If there are more students after "Z," return to the beginning of the alphabet.)

   You may wish to begin the activity by holding a whole-class discussion about the possible things that a child might see during a walk through the neighborhood. You may also alter the first sentence as desired. For example, you may begin, "In my house I saw a…," or "I went to the city and saw a…."

4. **Alphabet Name Game:** Give each student a soup bowl with alphabet macaroni or paper letters. Write a word on the board. The first student to spell the word with his/her alphabet letters is the winner of the round. Next, have students work in pairs to spell as many words as they can with their letters, making a written list of the words they spell. Beginning readers can spell their names by locating the appropriate alphabet letters. This activity increases letter recognition and spelling skills while at the same time introducing friendly competition. (You can also play noncompetitively.)

5. **Learn to Take Turns:** Explore the many ways of taking turns. For example, vote, flip coins, let a neutral party decide, draw straws, draw names, guess a number or a letter, or simply take turns being leader.

Whole-Classroom Readiness and Activities *(cont.)*

See page 7, "Shoe Hunt/Partner Hunt," for directions.

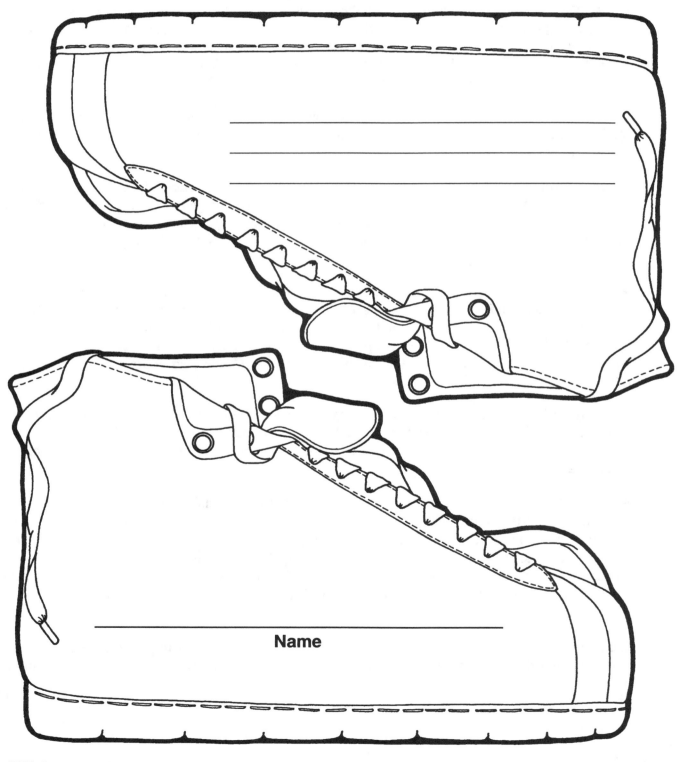

Name

Whole-Classroom Readiness and Activities (cont.)

6. **Picture Journal:** This activity can be used for individual and partner interaction. Have each child start a picture journal. When any classroom activity ends, have the children draw and write about the activity. Each journal entry can be dated with a notation about the activity to which it is referring.

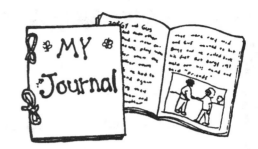

Let the students know that this journal is for them. There is no one right way to do it. It is just for fun. They can look back on it and remember what they did in class and how they felt about it.

Partners: Assign a partner to each child. Partners will discuss their journal entries. This activity will not only help children to relax in a cooperative learning environment, but it will also build cooperative and communicative skills in a nonthreatening way.

7. **Rest and Remember:** This activity will help children prepare for or unwind after a classroom activity or special event. Have the children go to their seats and rest their heads on their desks. You may wish to dim the classroom lights or play soft music. While the students are resting, ask them to think about the activity that they just completed. Ask them to picture the activity, see it as a mental movie, and decide what they liked and did not like about it. Ask them how they felt—happy, sad, angry, excited, etc. Ask them what they would like to do differently next time they work in their groups. You may then wish to follow up by reading to the students a short, happy poem or story.

Partners: Have students talk with a partner immediately following the "Rest and Remember" exercise, discussing what they liked about the activity they have just completed. This can also be another opportunity to use their picture journals.

8. **Letter Home:** This activity is helpful in encouraging language and memory skills. It also engenders parental and parent/child participation in your program.

Have students write and illustrate, or simply illustrate on a blank sheet of paper, what they did in a cooperative learning activity. Use the form on page 10 or have students create their own. Students can then take their letters home with the illustrations attached.

Have students return the letters to school and share what their parents said about the activity and their participation. These letters will also help you to stay in contact with parents consistently, rather than just when there is a problem.

Partners: Have partners view each others' letters home and make one positive comment or compliment. This activity encourages students to support each other, and it promotes self-esteem.

Whole-Classroom Readiness and Activities *(cont.)*

Dear_____,

Here is a picture of what my cooperative learning group did today.

I helped my group by...

_____

_____

My favorite part was...

_____

_____

Love,

_____

- -

Parent Comments:

_____

_____

Note from the Teacher: Thank you for supporting your child in his/her cooperative learning experience. I welcome all parent volunteers. Please write your number here if you would like a phone call.

Thank you,

_____

Name: _____

Name of Child: _____

Phone:_____

Selecting Cooperative Groups

Picture This

It is day one of a new school year. Mrs. Sumersover walks shakily into her classroom and gazes out at the sea of expectant, young faces. She feels stressed. She would like to add cooperative learning to her program this year, but she is not really sure how to do it. Most of her experience has been in traditional classroom settings. She spent the summer at the beach reading information on cooperative learning, but she still feels unsure and uncomfortable. She does not have tenure, the economy is in recession, and she can not afford to make any mistakes. At the same time, other teachers have already successfully incorporated cooperative learning into their classrooms. Mrs. Sumersover needs assistance from a friendly, clear, nonthreatening source.

I Need a Vacation!

Most of us are not this worried about how to incorporate current teaching trends into our classroom, but many of us have shared Mrs. Sumersover's sense of dread. Mrs. Sumersover needs a clear, concise, stress-free, and stimulating resource to help her pull her classroom and her curriculum together.

Icing on the Cake

Mrs. Gotabeperfect walks to her classroom on the first day of school. Eyes follow her. How does anyone who teaches manage to look that composed? She opens the door to her classroom with satisfaction. A giant fabric palm tree rises from the center of the room. Gleaming computers shine in a neat row against the wall, keyboards ready for little fingers. In one corner, a wooden reading area built to look like a real tree house stands like a monument to learning.

Top of the Class

She just needs one more thing: a cooperative learning plan as well-prepared and nifty as her inviting classroom. She needs cutting-edge materials to make her curriculum sparkle as much as her room does. She is a professional and a perfectionist, and she has to have the best.

Making It Happen

Maybe you know both of these teachers. Both of them could benefit from streamlined, easy, effective ways of incorporating cooperative learning into their classrooms successfully—the first time. The following pages give you quick and easy guidelines on how to set up your cooperative learning classroom. Blackline master forms have been included whenever possible to streamline the process.

Selecting Cooperative Groups *(cont.)*

Kinds of Learners

While all children are different, and certainly children's abilities and skill levels can change, most students fit into one of these four categories of learners:

• High Achievers	• Special Needs Students
• English as a Second Language (ESL) Students	• Competent Achievers

When selecting the members of cooperative groups, be sure to create a mix of all four areas. To help determine the members of each of your cooperative groups, the following descriptions offer some easily recognizable qualities that learners of the same type share.

High Achievers

High achievers can fall into two categories. Current educational thought holds that while some students are considered high achievers based on their I.Q., others are labeled this way not so much because of exceptional intelligence but because of exceptional motivation. When looking for the high achievers, consider these qualities:

• High I.Q.	• Good study and concentration skills	• Leadership skills
• Good verbal skills	• Academic excellence	• Exceptional talent
• Communication skills	• Interest in learning	• Multifaceted interests and abilities
• Problem-solving ability		

While there are certainly other ways to determine high achievers (and not all high achievers share the same qualities), this partial list will help you know what qualities to consider. High achievers can bring ideas, leadership, and assistance into a cooperative group.

Special Needs Students

While special needs students can be high achievers, low achievers, ESL, or English speaking, the commonality is that they all need special assistance. Some may have difficult family situations, (like a divorce or separation), while others may be diagnosed with severe emotional or behavioral problems. While the special needs student requires extra care, placing him/her in the right situation just might diminish or solve his/her problem. A sad, distracted child might be placed in a group with an outgoing, happy child, thus giving that child a model for growth. Children, like adults, benefit from the positive attitudes of those around them.

Look for these qualities when determining your special needs students:

• History of emotional or behavioral problems	• Recovery from a recent illness	• Quick frustration
• Anger	• A.D.D. student	• New to the area
• Low level of socalization skills	• Recent family upset	
	• Low motivation	

Selecting Cooperative Groups (cont.)

Special Needs Students (cont.)

While there are other things that may contribute to a child's place in the special needs category, these qualities will give you a guiding framework. Remember that this group, more than any of the others, is transitory. It is very possible during the length of a school year for a child's situation to change enough to either remove him/her or add him/her to this category.

English as a Second Language (ESL) Students

ESL students are usually challenged by the circumstances of their learning. Most of us have no idea how traumatic it is to be relocated to a new country with little or no knowledge of the language, the customs, the culture, or the people. Moreover, these students are often without friends, having left their companions behind.

ESL students come in every variety under the sun. Some are extremely well-educated in their own language, learn English quickly, and assimilate with relative ease. Others have frightening, painful experiences when it comes to success in their new schools.

ESL students have a special place in this book—one that will help you to help them to bring their own cultures into the learning experience. Instead of being ostracized for their differences by other students, they will be able to assume the role of "cultural diplomat." It is the intention of this book to support multicultural awareness and education wherever possible. The emphasis on cooperative learning in each unit makes the challenge of guiding ESL students toward success a little easier. When looking for students to classify as ESL, focus on the following characteristics:

- Recently arrived from another country
- American born but in a home where a language other than English is predominant
- Speaks English well but has not mastered reading or writing in English
- English speaking, but under the care of one for whom English is a second language
- Remains in the "silent interval" of language acquisition

Once provided with the special attention they need, ESL students often turn out to be competent or high achievers. The cooperative learning activities in this book will help you to access the strengths of these students and to provide them with many self-esteem building opportunities.

Competent Achievers

Unfortunately, competent achievers, often those who "do not give any trouble," just as often get very little teacher attention. In a classroom with 30 or more children, it is the competent child who is "all right" and gets left to fend for him/herself. When identifying competent achievers in your classroom, remember that these children should be rewarded and not penalized for being less demanding. Furthermore, in every group of competent achievers, there are a number of hidden high achievers who will blossom with the proper self-esteem-building attention and experiences.

Selecting Cooperative Groups *(cont.)*

Competent Achievers *(cont.)*

When looking for competent achievers, watch for the following signs:

- Students you do not often think about
- Average grades
- Oral and written language skills around grade level
- Shyness or quietness

- Pleasant, low-key personalities
- Low resistance to the learning experience
- A marked willingness to follow

While not all competent achievers fit this mold, it is at least safe to say that these are the children you are less likely to think about than any of the others. They are the children who stand in line, raise their hands, and rarely cause any disturbances. Competent achievers are the people who keep the world running smoothly, (in and out of the classroom), and for this they deserve much praise.

Now What?

Now that you know what to look for in determining the different learning types in your classroom, use page 15 to simplify the process.

As far as group size is concerned, five is a good number. Therefore, if you have thirty students, you will create six groups, each consisting of five individuals. In cooperative learning situations, an uneven number is an asset during the decision process. (No "hung jury," so to speak!)

Remember The "Salad Bowl"

Rather than as a melting pot, a situation in which everyone's individual traits melt together, the ideal cooperative learning situation should be thought of as a salad bowl. In a salad bowl, all ingredients (individual learning types) mix together. They create synergy while remaining individuals. Make a "cooperative learning salad bowl" in your classroom with this simple recipe:

1. Combine the following ingredients: high achievers, special needs students, ESL students, and competent achievers.

2. Select five according to taste. Flavor with the following random differences: genders, personality types, ethnicities, and learning styles.

Introduce each ingredient into the mix slowly, stirring in large pieces of humor, understanding, cooperation, and support. Let the mix remain together—qualities, strengths, and weaknesses intermingling. Facilitate ingredients rising to the occasion …and enjoy the results!

Selecting Cooperative Groups *(cont.)*

Legend

HA: High Achiever
SN: Special Needs Student
ESL: English as a Second Language Student
CA: Competent Achiever

Group One (example)	Group Two	Group Three
(HA)	( )	( )
(CA)	( )	( )
(CA)	( )	( )
(SN)	( )	( )
(ESL)	( )	( )
Notes:_____	Notes:_____	Notes:_____
_____	_____	_____
_____	_____	_____

Group Four	Group Five	Group Six
( )	( )	( )
( )	( )	( )
( )	( )	( )
( )	( )	( )
( )	( )	( )
Notes:_____	Notes:_____	Notes:_____
_____	_____	_____
_____	_____	_____

Parent Introduction Letter

Dear Parents,

In our classroom this year, we will be enriching our math curriculum in a very interesting way. We will be studying various math concepts by working cooperatively in pairs and in groups. This will give everyone a chance to take part in many enriching learning experiences.

Cooperative learning is a special kind of learning. Rather than sitting in a chair all day doing pencil-and-paper work, your child will be working in small groups, discussing ideas with other students. He/she will have the chance to get more personalized attention while learning to interact effectively with peers. Since the subject to be studied in these groups is math, students will have a real opportunity to practice thinking skills that are difficult to address in a conventional classroom situation.

Here is where you come in. Because of this different way of learning, parent volunteers are more important than ever. If you have several hours a week that you would like to spend in your child's classroom, it would be a wonderful help to the class, and it would also provide a very fond memory for your child.

I realize, of course, that most of you have extremely busy schedules and that some of you will not be able to take part in our classroom on a regular basis, but occasional drop-in helpers are appreciated too. There are also many other ways to take part in your child's learning experience, and I would be happy to talk with you about how you can become involved. Thank you for your support.

Sincerely,

_____

- -

If you would like me to call you, please fill in the information below and send it to me.

Name: _____

Child's Name: _____

Phone: _____

Assessment and Portfolios

Make It Manageable

Assessing your students' progress does not have to be a formidable task. Included for you here are two handy forms to lighten the load and consolidate your efforts. First, there is the "Individual Anecdotal Record" on page 18. Use this to keep a daily record of individual student progress in each activity or area. Make sure to date these records and to include them in a student portfolio. For more information and other forms, refer to Teacher Created Materials' *Portfolios and Other Assessments*.

Next, you will find "Reflections on the Activity" on page 19. This form is for students to fill out after each activity. Again, store them in their portfolios. This form will help you gauge how the students are doing and how they are feeling about the activities.

A Word About Portfolios

Create portfolios out of small boxes or shirt gift boxes, something that can stack but at the same time is big enough for bulky projects. It is important when assessing your students by the portfolio method to make parents aware that they will not receive as much take-home work. It is always a good idea to make parents aware of your assessment process and make them part of it at the very beginning of the year. Inform them every step of the way, and you will save yourself some big headaches. You may even get some interested and wonderful parent helpers.

Assessment and the Pre-Cooperative Learner

Finally, remember that cooperative learning is a difficult concept. Preschoolers and some primary children prefer, and are far better at, parallel play. The transition is usually a slow one. Keep in mind that it is a process and adjust your expectations accordingly.

Have Fun!

This book has been designed with the idea that not only will your students like the activities and have a good time, but so will you. Choose activities that you really love. Do not feel you have to do them all or that your must do them word for word. Together with your own creativity, the activities in this book will equal a fabulous year. Good luck!

Assessment and Portfolios *(cont.)*

Reproduce a stack of these forms and keep them—one for each student in your class—in a three-ring binder. Make your notes directly on the appropriate form. When a page is filled up, it can be replaced with a new page and the filled page placed in the student's portfolio. No time will be lost transcribing information.

Individual Anecdotal Record

Name _____

Date	Comment

Assessment and Portfolios *(cont.)*

Reproduce copies of this form for your students to use as they start the process of reflecting on their own achievements. This particular form was designed for primary children and requires little writing. Allow plenty of time for the children to look over and think about their work. When the form has been completed, attach it to the work (if possible) and include it in each student's portfolio.

Reflections on the Activity

Name _____ Date _____

When I look back on the work I have done, I feel...

I have become better at...

_____

_____

_____

_____

_____

I am really proud of...

_____

_____

Next time I do an activity like this, I will...

_____

_____

The Math Club Center

Centers Make Sense

In order to keep your cooperative math units running smoothly, as well as to lend an imaginative theme to your classroom and excite your students, we have designed a motivating Math Club Center for you to set up in your classroom. It will help to pull together your math units and provide a storage place for all of your supplies.

Before beginning, look at the list on page 21 and see what materials you will need to buy or perhaps have donated from parents or organizations. (See page 22 for a general "Parent Supply Letter." We have written this letter so that you can conveniently request the supplies you need.)

Everything Easy and Organized

This center works two ways. Its first function is to keep everything you use organized and in place. There is nothing more frustrating than beginning a cooperative activity and finding that a crucial part of the activity is missing. Besides being very frustrating for you, it makes the students unhappy and frustrated, and ruins the flow of an otherwise enjoyable and successful cooperative activity.

We have written each and every activity in this book to fit in a tub, such as a rectangular plastic dishpan, and each tub can be prepared and stored in the Math Club Center. You will want to make children accountable for keeping their Math Club Center neat and usable, and you will find that students become excited about the club theme.

Math Club Fun

The second function of this center is to make the Math Club theme accessible and exciting to your students. Having a "place" where it all happens is enjoyable for students and certainly showy for your room. In this center, there is a place to conduct demonstrations, a place to watch math videos and listen to audio tapes, and a place to get math books and to read them. All of these things add continuity to the units and importance to the ideas that the students are learning.

What You Need

To determine your Math Club center needs, read the information on page 21. Whenever possible, borrow or ask for donations. There are many things that can be requested from parents. Take advantage of the resources around you. Too many times teachers are hesitant to delegate, and they become totally responsible for making something work, taking on not only all of the leg work but also all of the expense.

The Math Club Center *(cont.)*

Supplies

- large table
- smaller display table
- chairs
- six plastic tubs such as rectangular dishpans (more, if possible, for preplanning)
- manipulatives (see list of suggestions on page 23)
- large closable plastic boxes
- bookshelves
- bulletin board space
- electric outlet
- television

- VCR
- tape recorder
- math tapes for the VCR
- blank tapes
- cleaning supplies
- paper towels
- construction paper
- crayons
- new pencils with erasers
- pencil cups
- one shirt-size gift box for each student (for portfolios)

These are the most general of the supplies you will find useful. Remember that a list of materials needed for each activity is provided at the beginning of that activity's text, as well as a picture of the stocked tub for the activity, for teachers who prefer to see a picture of how it should look. By seeing what is needed as well as reading a list, you will find it easier to set up your supplies for each activity quickly. (Additionally, the pictures will allow student helpers to assist you with the tub set-up, as you can simply say, "Make it look like this!")

Not Another Saturday!

This center will not take a whole Saturday to set up unless you want to get creative and play around with ideas as many teachers love to do. After compiling your materials, get an able-bodied helper and you should be able to put everything in place in less than an hour or two. (See the center floor plan on page 24.)

Remember to Use It

Even though it looks attractive and is an easy way to make your room look festive, the center is meant to remove as many organizational headaches from your day as possible. After each activity, have students replace what they have used. Get student helpers enrolled in tub set up. We have also included a place for portfolios to be stored where they will be very usable and accessible to your students. They can then take responsibility for the portfolios on whatever level you wish.

Preparation

Parent Supply Letter

Dear Parents,

We are busily setting up our Math Club Center and, in the interest of spending as little as possible of the money I have available for supplies, I am asking you to look around your home (and garage or storage area) for some of the items we need.

Here is the list I have put together:

large table	cleaning supplies
smaller display table	paper towels
chairs	construction paper
plastic tubs (like rectangular dishpans)	crayons
large closable plastic boxes	new pencils with erasers
bookshelves	pencil cups
math tapes for the VCR	plastic badge holders
tape recorders	shirt-size gift boxes
blank video and audio tapes	

We can also use scales of various kinds, measuring devices, and plastic containers of all shapes and sizes, as well as a variety of items to use as manipulatives (see the suggestions on the attached page).

If you have one or more of these items to spare, or if you could help pick up and deliver donations, please let me know. Any help will make our classroom more special. We plan to have an acknowledgement space on our bulletin board, recognizing your help and/or donations.

Thank you for your help.

Sincerely,

_____

- -

I can help! Please call me.

Name _____

Child's Name _____

Phone Number _____ Best Time to Call _____

Things to Use for Manipulatives

Manipulatives
Blocks
Bottle caps
Buttons
Candy
Gummy bears and worms
Chocolate candies
Candy corn
Chocolate drops
Jelly beans
Can tabs
Coins, especially pennies
Costume jewelry
Crayons
Dice
Dominoes
Dry beans, peas, etc.
Dry pasta in different shapes
Erasers
Game pieces
Jacks
Jigsaw puzzles
Keys
Plastic building blocks
Marbles
Paper clips
Pencils

Pipe cleaners
Play money
Playing cards
Rocks
Rubber bands
Shells
Spools
Straws
Poker chips
Tiles
Toy cars
Toys, small assorted

Containers
Baskets
Buckets
Butter tubs
Cardboard boxes
Coffee cans
Cookie cans
Gift bags
Margarine tubs
Oatmeal boxes
Pails
Plastic containers
Clear plastic, resealable bags in different sizes

Math Center Floor Plan

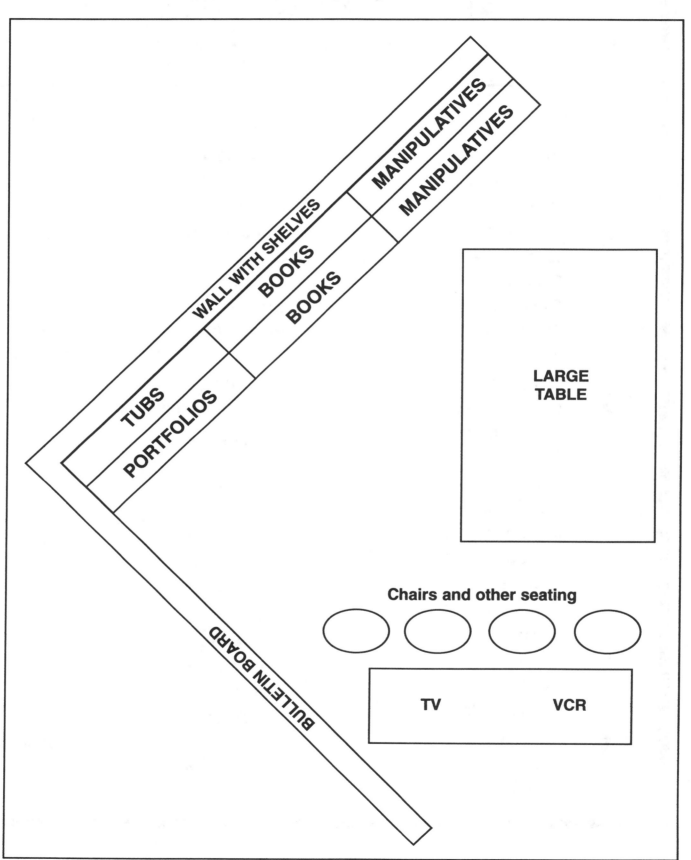

Math Club Membership Badges

How to Make Badges:

- Write the school name and the student's name on the lines.
- Cut out the badge. Laminate.
- Turn the badge over. On the back, tape a safety pin in the center.

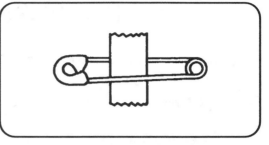

Back View

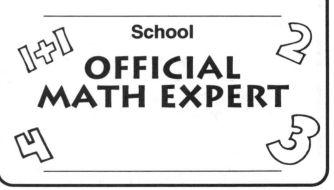

Getting to Know Me

Purpose: to establish rapport and a sense of comfort among the members of a cooperative group

Skills: communicating, using oral language, decision making, and listening

Materials Per Student: "Getting to Know Me Game" (page 28), "How We Work Together" (page 29), pencils or pens, and coloring materials

Procedures: As a class, go over the rules on "How We Work Together." These rules will let students know how to be effective members of a cooperative team. You can also enlarge the rules to poster size to display in the classroom.

Next, tell the children that they are going to get to know each other. Explain the simple information they will share by modeling the questions and answers on page 28. (See the teacher script on page 27.) Now, ask the students to sit in a circle in their cooperative groups. Give each student a copy of page 28. Students will answer the questions about themselves and share their answers with their individual groups. If possible, have each group work with an older student helper or a parent volunteer to assist them in this activity.

1. When we work in groups, we always take turns.

2. We listen when other people talk.

3. Everyone in the group gets to have a turn.

4. If we cannot agree on something, we vote.

5. If we have a problem, we try to work it out. We do not fight.

6. If we do not know what to do or we have a question, we ask the group first and then the teacher.

To Simplify: Have pre-cooperative learners sit with their groups and each think of his/her favorite food. Then, ask the students to listen to the favorite foods of each person in their group. Explain that a prize will go to the group whose members listen best and can tell what their "group's" favorite foods are. Offer the winning group something small like stickers or candy. This activity will enhance the listening and speaking skills of the pre-cooperative learner.

To Expand: Have advanced students share their "Getting to Know Me" pages and discuss their similarities and differences. Next, have them color their pages and make them into a book. Students may work together on a cover, thus creating their group's cover cooperatively.

Getting to Know Me *(cont.)*

Teacher Script: Today we are going to begin working in our groups. We are going to get to know each other and find out a little bit about each other. Before we start, let's go over our "How We Work Together" rules. (*Read the rules aloud.*) Let's talk about what these rules mean. (*At this point, let the children discuss the rules and give examples of what they mean.*) Good, now I think we are almost ready to start.

I need someone to play the "Getting to Know Me Game" with me to show the class how. Okay, Amber will help me. Everyone, please look at your paper. There are five statements. The first one says, "My favorite color is _____. I will tell Amber my favorite color, and then I will let her tell me her favorite color. We will both take turns talking and listening to each other, and we will try to remember each other's favorite color. When we work in our groups, everyone will get a turn to tell the rest of the group about his or her favorite color, and so forth. (*Model the activity.*)

Now let's all sit in our groups and give it a try. Your helper will help you get started and answer your questions. I will walk around the room and help you, too.

Evaluation and Processing: Evaluate this exercise by spending time with each group during the activity to see how they are doing. You will be able to gauge their success easily by interacting with each group. Process with your whole class by giving students a chance to share their group's answers and tell what they liked the most about the activity.

All About Me

My favorite color is blue.

My favorite food is pizza.

I have one brother and one sister.

My favorite animal is a horse.

Name _____

Getting to Know Me Game

Complete these statements. When everyone is finished, tell your group your answers and listen to theirs.

1. My favorite color is _____.

2. My favorite food is _____.

3. I have _____ brother(s) and _____ sister(s).

4. My favorite toy is _____.

5. My favorite animal is _____.

Use this space to draw a picture about some of your statements.

How We Work Together

1. When we work in groups, we always take turns.

2. We listen when other people talk.

3. Everyone in the group gets to have a turn.

4. If we cannot agree on something, we vote.

5. If we have a problem, we try to work it out. We do not fight.

6. If we do not know what to do or we have a question, we ask the group first and then the teacher.

Compliment Letters

Reproduce and cut out a stack of these forms. A student may fill one out and give it to another student after an activity in order to positively support his/her partner. This activity encourages students to support each other and promotes self-esteem.

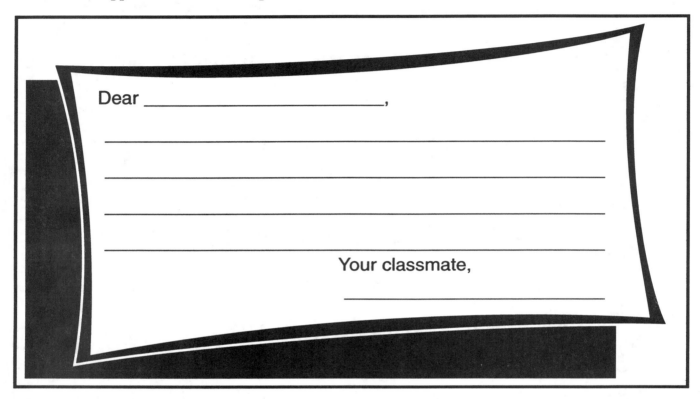

Dear _____,

_____

_____

_____

_____

Your classmate,

_____

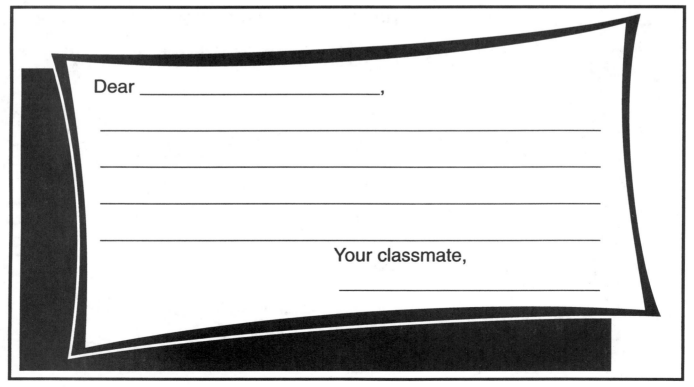

Dear _____,

_____

_____

_____

_____

Your classmate,

_____

Compliment Slips

Reproduce this page. Cut out the slips and distribute them to positively support students' progress.

Great Idea!	**Wow!**
NICE JOB!	**You are very cooperative!**
I like your attitude!	**You really worked hard!**
Super!	**Neat!**
You should be proud!	**Terrific!**

Observing and Sorting

Purpose: to define, discuss, and apply the idea of attributes by observing and sorting collections of objects

Skills: following directions, cooperating, using oral and written language skills

Mathematical Skills: observing characteristics of objects, sorting objects by a variety of characteristics

Materials: for each group—a different collection of objects (buttons, shells, small colored blocks, assorted beads, small toy figures, crayons, etc.), "Attributes" activity sheet (one per group plus extras), sharpened pencils for writing

Procedures: Students work in groups to observe and describe the attributes of a collection of objects. Begin this activity by holding a whole-class discussion of attributes. Define *attributes* (characteristics or qualities) for students. Use the students in your classroom as examples. Ask students to make suggestions which you can record on the chalkboard. You should arrive at a list of attributes such as the ones appearing on the "Attributes" activity sheet on page 34.

After the whole-class discussion, have students take their math tubs and move to their cooperative groups. Have them pour their collection of objects out and look at them as they fill out the "Attributes" page. Remind them to write down all of their observations. When all groups have completed their activity sheets, have them meet together as a large group for a discussion. Ask each group to read the special attributes they have recorded under the heading "Other." (The group with buttons may specify the number of holes, for example.)

When all groups have shared, collect and save the activity sheets for the next activity.

To Simplify: Have children work with an older student or parent helper who will help them discuss and record their findings as they go along.

To Expand: Have students try to think of additional categories of attributes and write them on the back of the "Attributes" activity sheet.

Observing and Sorting *(cont.)*

Teacher Script: Today you are going to work in your cooperative groups to observe and describe the attributes of a collection of objects. But first of all, let's talk about attributes. Attributes are the characteristics or qualities things have. We can use attributes to talk about things that are the same or things that are different. For example, look around at the students in our classroom. What attributes do all of us have? Right! Size is an attribute. Some of us are tall and some are short. Color is an attribute. (*Continue in this manner, recording students' suggestions on the chalkboard. Encourage discussion.*)

Now please take your math tubs and move to your cooperative groups. Pour your collection of objects out and look at them. Use your "Attributes" activity sheet to write down all of your observations. When all the groups have completed their activity sheets, we will meet together as a large group for a discussion. Someone from each group will read the special attributes they may have recorded under the heading "Other."

When all groups have shared, remember to give me the activity sheets to save for the next activity.

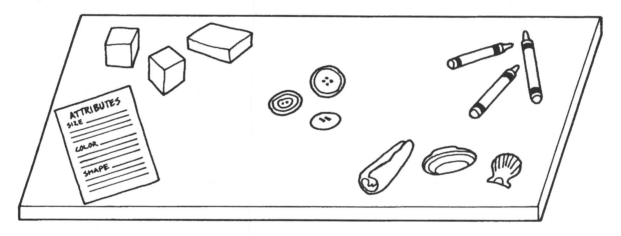

Evaluation and Processing: Have each group tell about their experiences and discuss the process with the whole class. Ask such questions as these: Did you write attributes for each heading? Did you think of some special attribute to write under the heading "Other?" Was this activity easy or hard? Did everyone in the group agree on all the attributes? Remember to use anecdotal record forms (page 18) to keep a record of participation for each child for each activity.

Group Name _____

Attributes

These are the attributes we observed:

Size _____

_____

_____

Color _____

_____

_____

Shape _____

_____

_____

Material _____

_____

_____

Other _____

_____

_____

_____

Math in a Tub Layout

Attributes

Guess the Rule

Purpose: to construct and solve puzzles based on knowledge of attributes

Skills: following directions, cooperating, inferring

Mathematical Skills: observing characteristics of objects, sorting objects by a variety of characteristics, making generalizations

Materials: for each group—a different collection of objects (buttons, shells, small colored blocks, assorted beads, small toy figures, crayons, etc.), several copies of page 37, pencils, string

Procedures: Make a large circle on the classroom floor using the string. Decide on a general attribute, such as "girls with blonde hair." Ask for volunteers and, one at a time, place them inside or outside your circle—girls with blonde hair inside, all others outside the circle. Ask students to guess what your general rule is. Repeat the process, using a different general attribute rule.

After the whole-class demonstration, have students take their math tubs and move to their groups. Have them use the "Attribute Puzzle" pages to plan several puzzles of their own. Next, have the members of the groups rotate so that they all have a chance to present their puzzles and to solve the puzzles of the other groups.

To Simplify: Have children work with an older student or parent helper who will help them plan and test their puzzles.

To Expand: Have students experiment with overlapping circles to make their puzzles more difficult.

Teacher Script: Today you are going to make up "Attribute Puzzles" based on rules you agree upon in your groups. First, I will use people in our classroom to demonstrate a puzzle based on my secret rule. I will make a circle on the classroom floor using this string. Raise your hand if you would like to be part of my puzzle. The rest of you watch carefully to see if you can figure out my secret rule.

Jan, you will stand outside the circle. (*Jan has dark hair.*) Sean will stand outside the circle too. (*Sean is a boy.*) Mary Lee will stand inside the circle. (*Mary Lee has blonde hair.*) Raise your hand as soon as you know what my rule is. (*Continue until someone comes to the correct conclusion—girls with blonde hair. Repeat, using a different general attribute rule.*)

Now you may take your math tubs and move to your cooperative groups. Use your "Attribute Puzzle" worksheets to plan several puzzles of your own. Write your general rule at the top of the puzzle sheet and complete the puzzle for practice. When every group has planned several puzzles, I will tell you how to move around the room and solve one another's puzzles. You can make a string circle on your table or borrow a hula hoop from the P.E. equipment.

Evaluation and Processing: Have each group tell about their experiences. Use anecdotal record forms (page 18).

Group Name _____

Attribute Puzzle

General Rule _____

_____

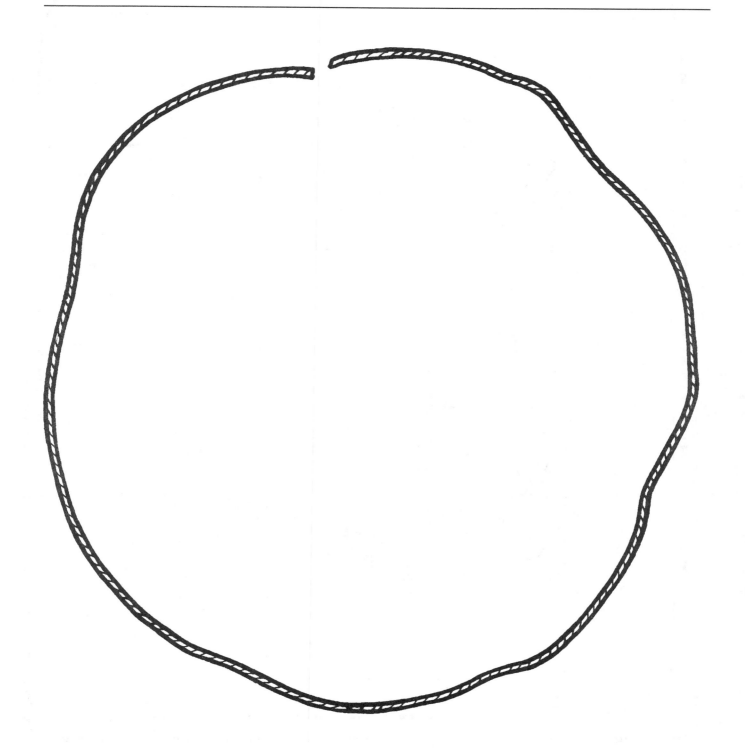

Math in a Tub Layout

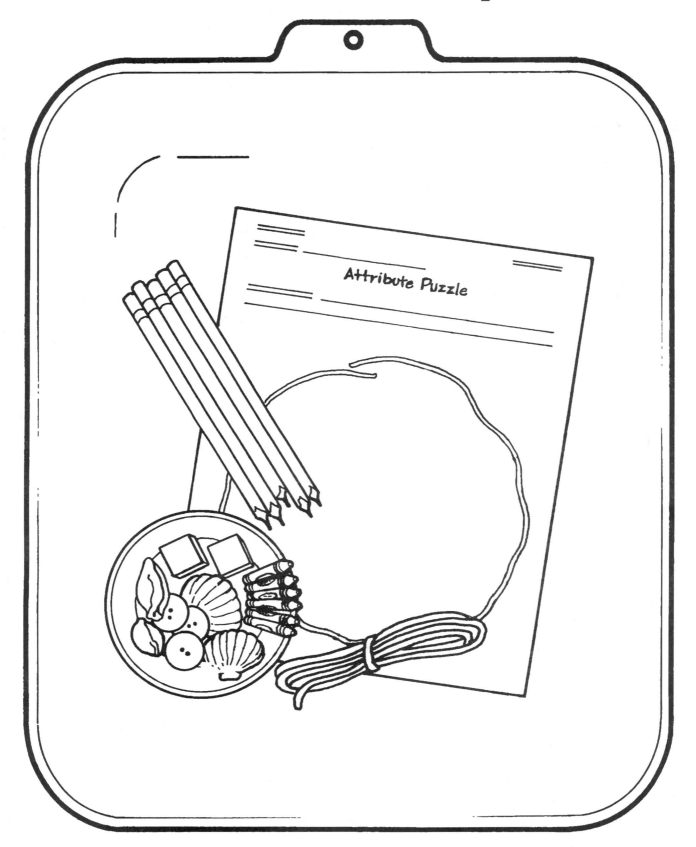

Attribute Puzzle

Games, Rules, and Playing Fair

Purpose: to learn the concept of playing a game, understand how to follow basic rules, take turns, and understand basic strategy

Skills: following directions, fairness, cooperation, and verbal skills

Mathematical Skills: logic, probability and statistics, adding and subtracting

Materials: for each group—one resealable plastic bag containing game items (see page 40), a copy of pages 41 and 42, one game board and spinner (pages 42 and 43), pencils

Procedures: Begin this activity by holding a whole-class discussion about games. Ask students to list their favorite games. Discuss how they are played. Work together to create whole-class "Playing Fair Rules" (page 44). Establish that these should be followed whenever they play games in your classroom.

Have students play the game. Use this simple game to acquaint your cooperative groups with the game-playing process again and again.

To Simplify: Replace the whole-class activity by having students work in cooperative groups to talk about playing fair. Then have students play the game.

To Expand: Have students expand the idea of playing fair across the curriculum. Have groups discuss and share situations when they felt that others were not playing fair, or write and relate stories about fairness.

Teacher Script: Today we are going to talk about playing games. We already play a lot of games in our classroom and at recess. Let's talk about what is important to remember when we are playing games. (*Discuss.*) Now we are going to make our very own classroom rules for playing games. Look at this poster. We will make five rules, and we will follow these rules when we play games. Let's think of ideas which are important to remember when we play games. (*Hold a whole-class discussion and create a whole-class rule poster to use whenever games are played in the classroom.*)

Please take your team's math tub and move to your group area. We are all going to play the game called the "Playing Fair Game." This is what everyone should have and how the game is played (*model activity*). Now let's all play the game in our cooperative groups. After we are finished, we will talk about it.

Evaluation and Processing: Have each group tell the whole class what happened when they were playing the game and how it turned out. Use anecdotal record forms (page 18) to record student participation.

Putting Together the Playing Fair Game

Use the following materials and directions to assemble the game.

Materials

- one copy of the game board on page 42 for each student group, enlarged to 11" x 14" (27.5 cm x 35 cm)
- red, blue, and yellow crayons or thick marking pens
- laminating paper
- scissors
- one brad for each spinner
- five game pieces for each game board
- dice for each game set
- one spinner for each game board (See page 43.)
- one resealable plastic bag for each game set

Teacher Directions

Making the "Playing Fair Game" is not difficult and does not require a great deal of time to prepare. You will want to gather the materials ahead of time and make all the games at once. The main idea is to make your games as sturdy and durable as possible so they can be used again and again by your students.

To begin, make enough copies of the game board on page 42 for each of your student groups. You will want to enlarge these copies. (Make the copies needed for the spinners at the same time. You will want to use a heavy stock paper for both of these, if possible.) An 11" x 14" (27.5 cm x 35 cm) game board makes a nice size. Next, color the spaces according to the color names listed on the board. Then laminate these boards with laminating paper to ensure that they will last.

Next, cut out the spinners and color the spinner sections as listed by color. Attach the spinner with the brad. Gather five game pieces for each game. (Use items which are small and easy to handle, such as buttons, coins, small discarded costume jewelry pieces, small rocks, or shells.) You will have to purchase dice for each set if you do not have them on hand in your classroom. Finally, place all the small items for each game in a resealable plastic bag. Place these in your math tubs. Now you are ready to prepare the rest of the materials for the tub. See the tub layout on page 45.

The Playing Fair Game

How to Play the Game

1. Put the game board on a table.

2. Have everyone pick a game piece and put it at "Start."

3. Decide whether you want to play "Colors" or "Numbers" first.

To Play "Colors"

1. Use the spinner.

2. Take turns spinning the spinner and move your game piece to the color.

3. Keep going until someone gets to the end of the game board.

4. That person wins!

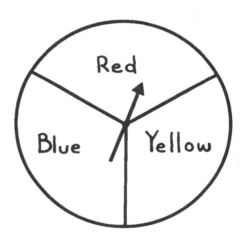

To Play "Numbers"

1. Use the dice.

2. Take turns—throw the dice and count the spaces to put your game piece on the right space.

3. Keep going until someone gets to the end of the game board.

4. That person wins!

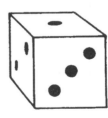

Playing Fair Game Board

Start here ↑	Y	R	B
R	B	Y	R
Y	R	B	Y
B	Y	R	B
R	B	Y	R
Y	R	B	Y
B	Y	R	B
R	B	Y	You win! ★

42

Spinner Masters

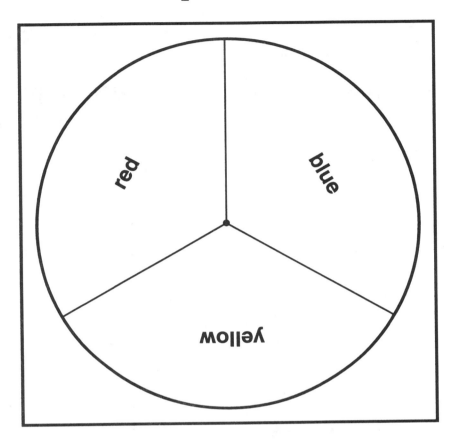

Attach spinner
arm with brad.

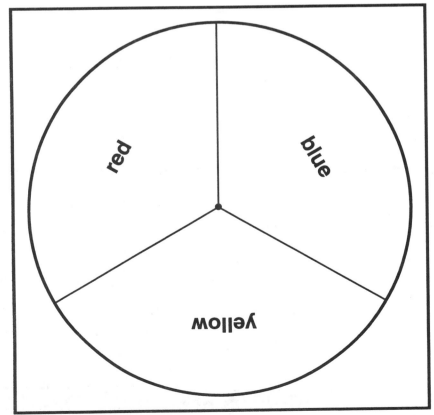

Playing Fair Rules

We, the students in _____ class, have
agreed that these are our "Playing Fair Rules."

1. _____
   _____

2. _____
   _____

3. _____
   _____

4. _____
   _____

5. _____
   _____

Signatures: _____

_____

_____

_____

Math in a Tub Layout

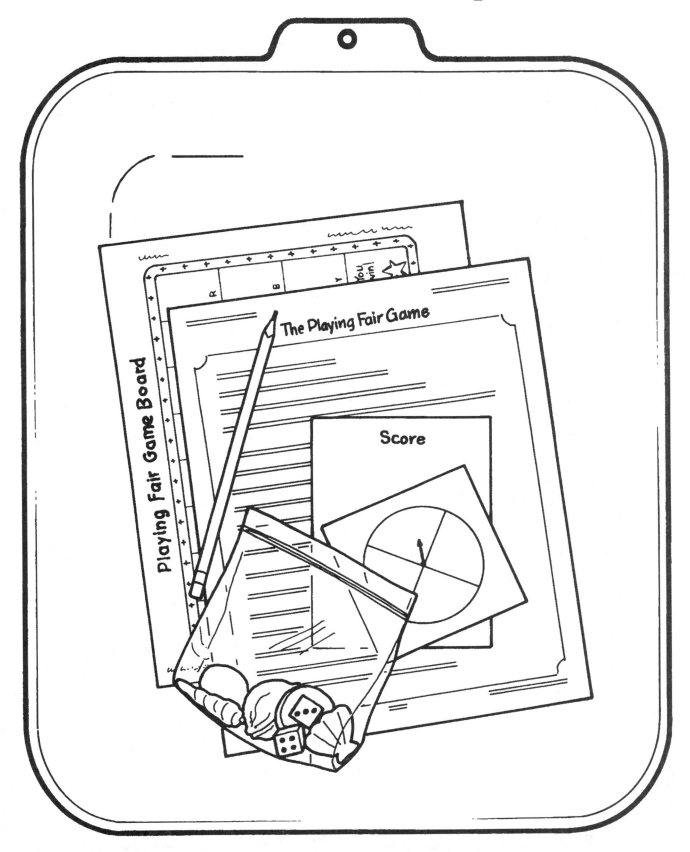

Making a Game

Purpose: to use game-playing skills learned in the previous activity to invent and play a simple game

Skills: decision making, imagination and creativity, cooperation and reaching consensus, communication, fairness

Mathematical Skills: logic, probability and statistics, adding and subtracting

Materials: for each group—a copy of pages 48 and 49, spinner, pencils, resealable plastic bag containing dice and game pieces, an 8" x 11" (20 cm x 28 cm) or 12" x 18" (30 cm x 46 cm) piece of construction paper or other heavy paper to be used as a game board

Procedures: To begin this activity, have teams review what they learned in the "Playing Fair Game" (pages 39–45). Next, explain to students that they will be using a game board and materials to make their own game.

Depending on the level of your students, this game will be either less or more complicated. (Children are always inventing games, even from a very early age. This exercise is simply an extension of that, adding mathematical ideas and organization to something they often already do.)

Engage students in a whole-class discussion about the kinds of games the children have already invented or played. Ask students to explain the rules and procedures of simple playground games.

To Simplify: Set an objective for the game that the students are going to invent. For example, each group will use a spinner and game pieces, and the player who moves his or her game piece around the board first wins. Setting some parameters of this kind will give the students a place to start.

To Expand: Have a game week. Carry the concept of games into all subject areas in your classroom curriculum. Have students play organized games at recess and during the lunch hour.

Devise ways for games to enter into other areas of learning. Guessing games are a possibility in history or language arts. "Twenty Questions" works well in science.

At the end of the week, have students write short stories telling about their favorite games.

Making a Game *(cont.)*

Teacher Script: Today we are going to play another game. But this will be a very special game! This will be a game you make up yourselves. Let's talk about what kinds of games we like to play, and especially what kinds of games we have made up or invented that are lots of fun. (*Hold class discussion.*)

Now every team will have a math tub full of game equipment. (*Model use of the supplies and the purpose of each.*) Now let's all move into our groups and talk about what kind of a game we would like to make. Use the "Making Your Own Game" activity sheet, and I will help you if you need help.

For this activity, each team will have one of our helpers to make it more fun. Let's give it a try. (*You may find that the addition of a student or parent helper for this activity will be fun and will give each team personal attention during the process of creating their own game.*)

After we make our games, we will play them. If we don't finish making our games today, we will finish them tomorrow.

Evaluation and Processing: After teams complete their games, spend time with the groups discussing the games and letting groups demonstrate them to you. Keep records on the anecdotal form on page 18.

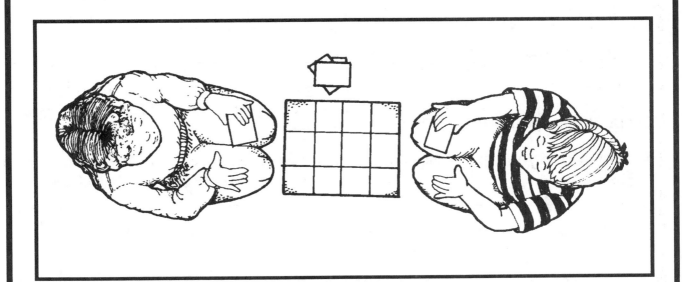

Making Your Own Game

Group Member Names:

_____

_____

Making your own game is fun! Work together to plan your own game here.

1. As a group, brainstorm your ideas for a game. (Use a brainstorm sheet or the back of this page for your ideas.)

2. What will be the object of your game? (How does someone win?)

   _____

3. What materials do you need for your game?

   _____

   _____

4. What are the rules for your game?

   Rule One_____

   _____

   Rule Two_____

   _____

   Rule Three _____

   _____

Now play your game and see how it works.

5. How does your game work?

   _____

6. What would make it better?

   _____

   _____

Blank Game Cards

Math in a Tub Layout

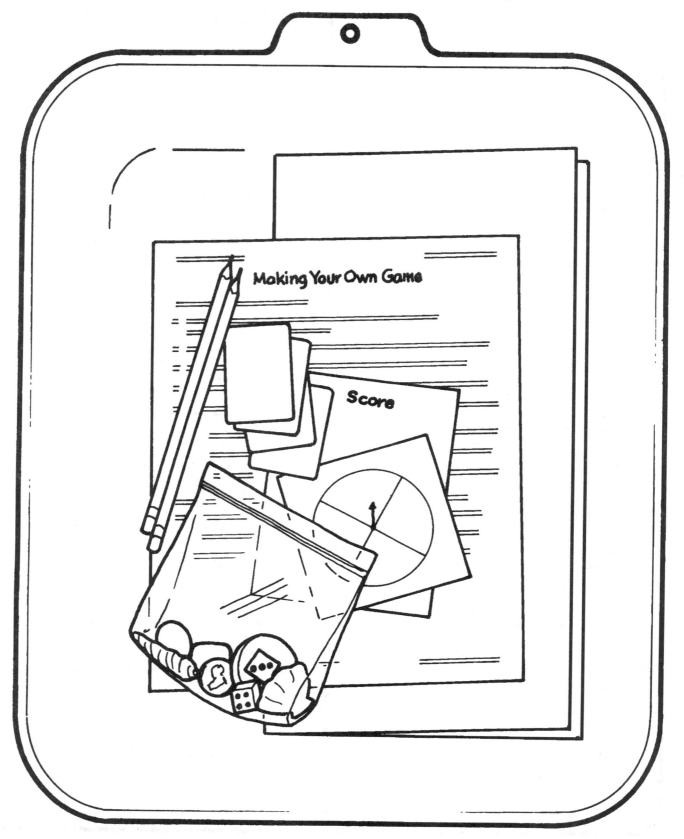

Making Your Own Game

Score

Number Hunt

Purpose: to become familiar with how numbers are used in everyday life and how they are important to our world

Skills: communicating, decision making, analytical thinking, sharing, brainstorming

Mathematical Skills: understanding number and numeration concepts, counting, one-to-one correspondence, understanding number symbols and their equivalents

Materials: for each group—one copy of pages 53 and 54, one copy of page 55 for each member of the group, tape measures, pens, rulers

Procedures: In this activity, students begin to see the importance of numbers in their daily lives by exploring the numbers around them. Begin this activity by illustrating the various important numbers in people's lives. A variety of examples include phone numbers and addresses, emergency numbers to call, numbers to find things, numbers to count things, and numbers to divide things fairly.

Begin this activity by holding a whole-class discussion about important numbers. Write examples that students think of on the board during the discussion. Ask students to begin to think about how they use numbers every day so that they can talk about this subject when they are in their cooperative groups.

Next, have students move to their cooperative groups and use the "Number Brainstorming Activity Sheet" to think of and write down as many ways as possible that they use numbers in their daily lives. Then take some time to discuss these lists with each group or have an older student helper or parent volunteer discuss what the children have thought of and give them some additional ideas and feedback.

Have children complete the "Number Hunt Group Activity Sheet." Some teachers may wish to make the number hunt a game. In this case, ask the first group finished to raise their hands, declare them the winner, and give them a prize. Other teachers will simply ask students to complete the activity sheet in their cooperative groups without making it a competition. For this part of the activity, students will use the measuring tools listed in the tub materials section.

To Simplify: Simplify this activity by having students complete one but not both of the cooperative group activity sheets. Or divide this activity into two activities, using each one on a separate day.

To Expand: Use the "My Important Numbers" activity sheet to emphasize safety issues, and focus a unit of several days on the importance of being able to get help in an emergency and how numbers play a part in that. This take-home activity sheet can easily introduce a unit on safety and emergencies.

Number Hunt *(cont.)*

Teacher Script: Today we are going to learn about why numbers are important in our lives. Let's take a quick look around the room for numbers. How many do we see? What do they tell us? Let's look at an example we have in our homes—a telephone. This telephone has numbers on it, and when you want to make a call, you need to know a phone number. How many of you know your own phone number? Great. Now let's make a list on the board of ways that we use numbers every day. After we have thought of a few ideas, we will move into our groups and think of as many more as we can. (*Ask for ideas and write a few on the board.*) Let's all move into our groups now. When you think of an idea, talk it over with your team and write it on your team activity sheet. I will walk around the room to help you. Okay, let's go.

Now let's stop and discuss the ideas we thought of (*whole-class discussion*). In a minute we will go back into our groups and play an exciting game called "Number Hunt." The first group to finish their "Number Hunt" activity sheet will win a prize. Let's all look at the activity sheet together first. (*Model worksheet and activity.*) Let's go. Remember, when your team finishes, have your messenger bring me your completed worksheet. Ready! Start!

Evaluation and Processing: End the activity by reviewing the results as a whole class and have each student fill out his/her personal number activity sheet to take home. Emphasize calling 911 and let each student try it on a pretend telephone (or one that is unplugged). Remind students that they must never call 911 unless an emergency occurs. Use the anecdotal record form on page 18 to log individual performance results.

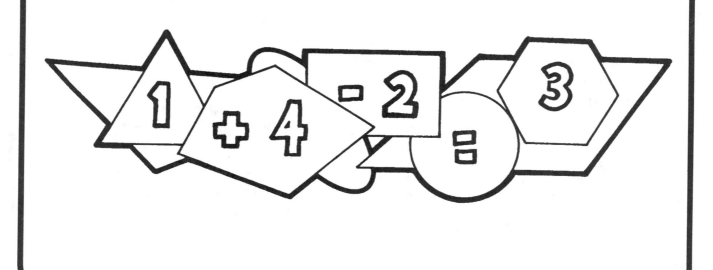

Number Brainstorming
Activity Sheet

Group Member Names:

_____

_____

What numbers do we see in our classroom? Tell about them here:

1. _____

2. _____

3. _____

4. _____

5. _____

6. _____

7. _____

8. _____

9. _____

10. _____

11. _____

12. _____

What numbers do we see outside our classroom? Tell about them on the back of this paper.

Number Hunt
Group Activity Sheet

Group Member Names:

_____

_____

We use numbers everyday! Find answers for these number questions!

1. What are the ages of the students in your group?

    _____

    _____

2. How tall are the students in your group?

    _____

    _____

3. What is the number for the day each student in your group was born?

    _____

    _____

4. What numbers do you see in our classroom that help us everyday?

    _____

5. Go outside your classroom with your teacher or aide and look for
    numbers. What numbers do you see outside? Write some of them on
    the lines below. Then, on the back of this paper tell how the numbers
    help us.

    _____   _____

    _____   _____

    _____   _____

    _____   _____

My Important Numbers

Name _____

What is my address?

_____

_____

_____

What is my phone number?

_____

How old am I?

_____

When is my birthday?

_____

How tall am I?

_____

What number do I call in an emergency?

_____

What is my mother's or father's work number?

_____

What is my best friend's or neighbor's phone number?

_____

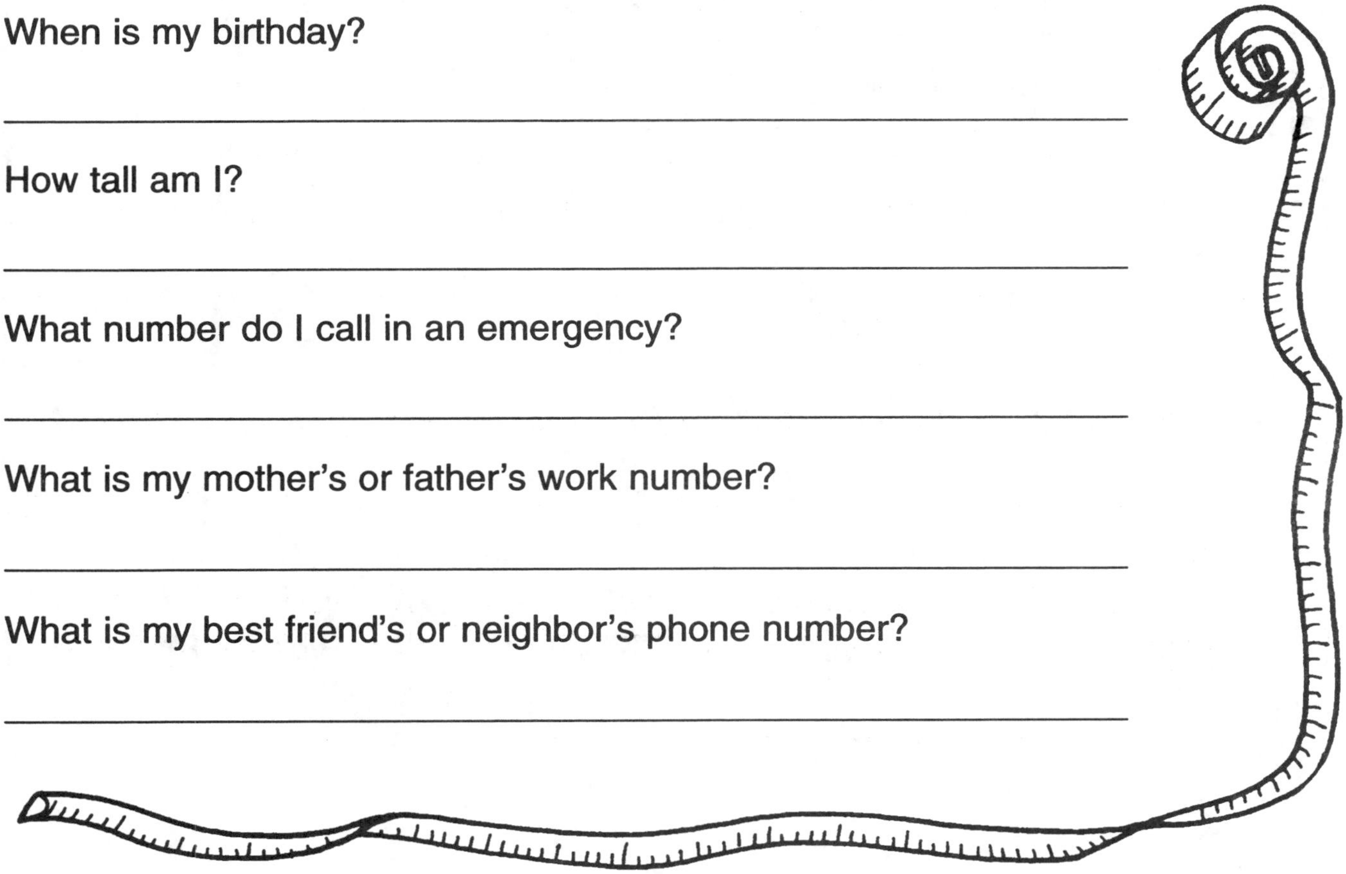

Math in a Tub Layout

Group Number Murals

Purpose: to become familiar with numbers and their equivalents through the process of creating a group number mural

Skills: cooperation, creativity, teamwork, decision making, reaching consensus, delegation

Mathematical Skills: understanding the concept of numerical representation to concretely represent amounts, using numbers to represent quantities

Materials: for each group—mural paper, art supplies, student pages 60–64, candy counters

Procedures: (**Note:** Some teachers may wish to divide this activity into small activities over a period of several days.) This activity can easily be divided into three days as follows:

> **Day One:** "Count Your Candy"
>
> **Day Two:** "Set Activity Sheet," "Number Mural Blank"
>
> **Day Three:** Large-group Set Mural

In this activity students become familiar with numbers and the quantities they represent by making a team number mural. Begin this activity by asking students to sit in their groups and play a number-grouping game. Give each student a handful of candy. Ask students to separate the candy into piles of one, two, three, four, and five. Then ask students to eat one out of each pile and count how many they have left, etc. Have students group various small objects into different quantities. Ask them to then express the number in different ways. For example, five is expressed as five gummy bears or three gummy bears and two candy corns. See how many different ways student groups can illustrate a specific number.

Next, have student groups use the small group mural practice sheet to make pictures of sets of things for each number, one through ten. Let students work together to use this small mural planning sheet to decide what kind of pictures they will have on their larger group mural. Ask students to think of simple things they can draw, and then draw the right amount for each section in the practice mural. For example, they might draw one flower for the "one" section. In the "two" section, they might draw two stars. Have them work together to make their practice mural, and remind them they will use this small mural to decide what they will do on their larger mural.

After students have completed their small practice murals, take time to work with each student group to make sure they have an understanding of the concept of creating a set for each number and then transferring it to a larger mural.

Group Number Murals *(cont.)*

To Simplify: Use the practice mural for the actual activity. Have student groups work together to complete the small practice mural. Forego the other steps of the activity.

To Expand: Use the "Number Snake" master on page 64 to expand the idea of representing numbers. This page is numbered in sections of ten. Decide, based on the level of the students you are working with, how high you would prefer the list to go. It has been created for use from 1–100 or anywhere in between. Use this number snake to have students represent simple mathematical problems. For example, on a number snake from one to ten, have students place a candy on each space. Then have them do simple subtraction. (Candy-eating subtraction problems are always more fun!) You can try a variety of math problems this way. Have advanced students experiment writing and eating their own math problems and then writing about their own problems to show you their progress. Additionally, students can then use the number snake to work other students' problems. This way they can work in pairs or cooperatively.

Teacher Script: Today we are going to have more fun using numbers! In our last activity we learned how numbers are very important in our lives and what we use them for everyday. Today we are going to learn about sets and using numbers to count, add, and subtract. Everyone will really like the very first thing we are going to do! We are going to play Candy Math! Candy Math is something everyone will like to do because first we figure out a math problem and then we eat it!

> **Day One:** First I will give every student a handful of candy. Remember, don't eat it yet. We have to do our math first! Okay, now everyone count out five gummy bears and put them in a pile. Good. Now let's all eat three gummy bears. How many do we each have left? Two! Now let's eat one. Now we have one left. I will write these problems on the chalkboard so we can see what we just did.
> (*Write: 5-3=2, 2-1=1*)

Group Number Murals *(cont.)*

Teacher Script *(cont.)*:

Day One: *(cont.)* Let's try a few more candy problems. Can anyone think of a problem to write on the board? We will work the problem using our candy. (*Have student volunteers try a variety of candy problems, and then have students work in cooperative groups trying more candy problems.*)

Now let's all move into our cooperative groups and work together to complete our "Count Your Candy" sheet. Remember to work all the math problems you write, using candy. I will walk around to see how you are doing.

Day Two: Today we are going to talk about sets. Can anyone tell me what a set is? A set is a group of things that go together. Let's think of some sets in our classroom. We can have a set of blocks or a set of letters or a set of toys. Let's look around and talk about it. (*Have group discussion with class regarding sets.*) Now, let me show you what we are going to do. Today we are going to make a mini-mural like this. (*Model activity using mural example on page 63.*)

When you go to your group today, after you complete your group worksheet, you will be making a mini-mural like this. Let's take a look at this. You see there are ten spaces numbered one through ten. Your team will think of ten sets of things and draw pictures in each of the spaces. Let's take a look at this example. What do we see in the space for "one"? That is right—we see one flower. Let's talk about the other spaces. (*Encourage whole-class discussion.*) Okay, let's move to our groups and complete our worksheets and our mini-murals. Let me know if you need help.

Day Three: Today we are going to take our mini-mural and copy it on a big mural. Every team will have a large sheet of butcher paper and a place on the floor to work. You will need to split up the tasks. In other words, decide who will draw which part of the mural and give everyone a job.

After all the murals are finished, we will put them up in the classroom and they will look really beautiful!

Evaluation and Processing: Review the three days of activities with your class, both on a daily basis and after the entire activity is completed. Use the anecdotal record form (page 18) and the student "Reflections on the Activity" (page 19) to get a sense of what students learned from the activity. Make sure to date the forms.

Count Your Candy

How many pieces of candy does each person have?

Name   **How Many?**

1. _____   _____

2. _____   _____

3. _____   _____

4. _____   _____

5. _____   _____

Each member of your group should write a math problem for your group to try here. After you have finished, work the problem using candy.

1. _____

2. _____

3. _____

4. _____

5. _____

Set Activity Sheet

Group Members:

_____

_____

| **A set is a group of things that go together.** |

Decide what belongs in each of these sets.

See whether there is something missing or something that does not fit.

Talk about each set together and decide what to add or take away.

1. What is missing?

    (a set of gloves)   (a set of numbers, 1–10)

_____   _____

(a set of all the letters of the alphabet)

_____

2. What does **not** belong in this set? _____

Number Mural Blank

5	10
4	9
3	8
2	7
1	6

Number Mural Example

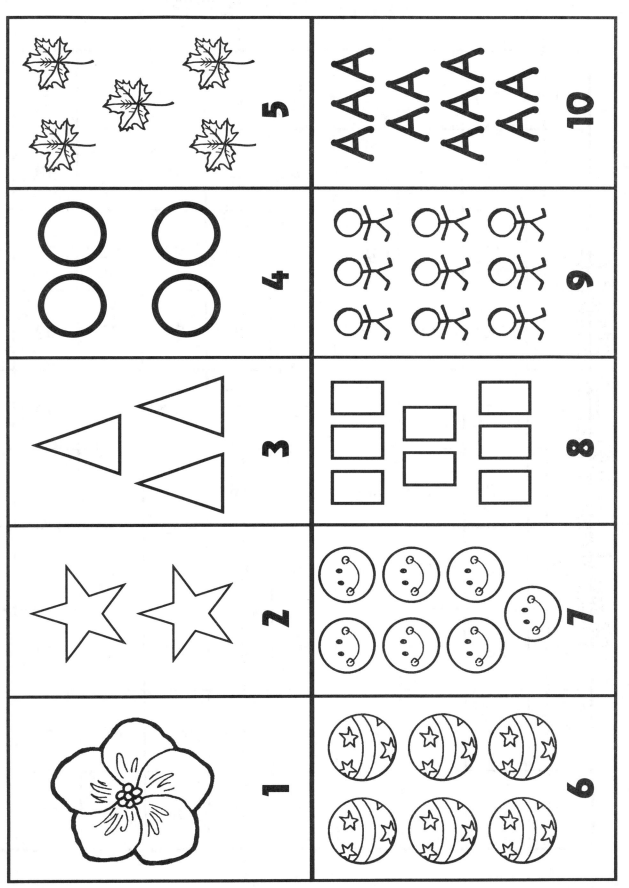

Number Snake

1	2	3	4	5	6	7	8	9	10
11	12	13	14	15	16	17	18	19	20
21	22	23	24	25	26	27	28	29	30
31	32	33	34	35	36	37	38	39	40
41	42	43	44	45	46	47	48	49	50
51	52	53	54	55	56	57	58	59	60
61	62	63	64	65	66	67	68	69	70
71	72	73	74	75	76	77	78	79	80
81	82	83	84	85	86	87	88	89	90
91	92	93	94	95	96	97	98	99	100

Math in a Tub Layout

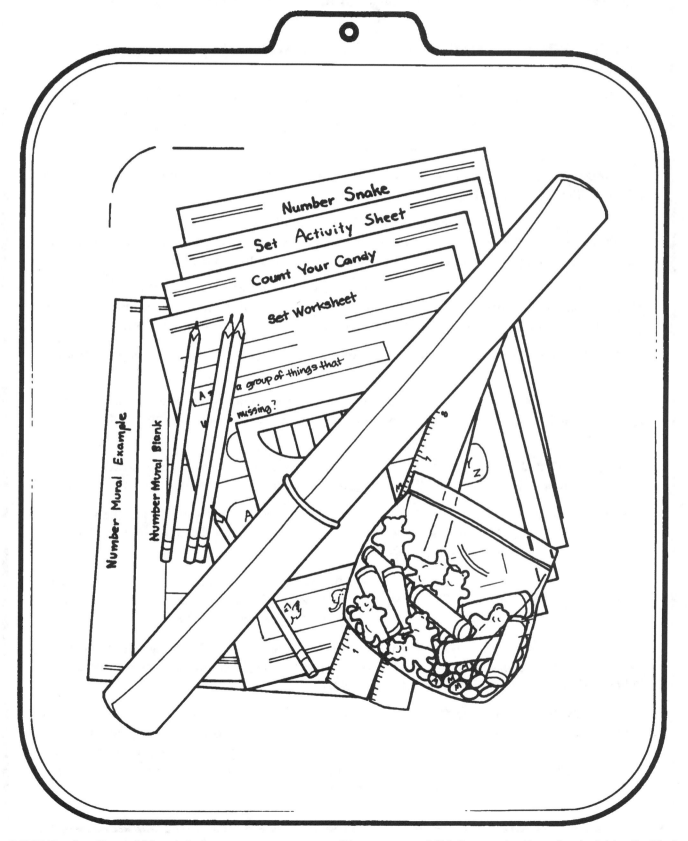

Addition Acts/Subtraction Skits

Purpose: to act out original solutions to given word problems in addition and subtraction

Skills: following directions, cooperating, using oral and written language, creativity

Mathematical Skills: comprehension of word problems, ability to formulate and dramatize solutions to given problems

Materials: for each group—a different "Word Problems" sheet, several word problem "Script Sheets" (with extras available), pencils

Procedures: Begin this activity by holding a whole-class demonstration. Read a sample word problem in addition or subtraction. Ask volunteers to help solve it and create a skit that dramatizes the solution. Show them how to use the "Script Sheet."

Next, have students move to their cooperative groups with the math tubs. When everyone has finished, have students meet in the large group to take turns reading their problems and giving their skits. Each group can choose a favorite skit to present to the class.

To Simplify: Have an older student or parent-volunteer assist each group in creating an appropriate skit.

To Expand: Have students write their own word problems to solve and dramatize. As a variation, each group can write word problems for other groups to solve and dramatize.

Teacher Script: Today you will work in your groups to solve some word problems in addition and subtraction and create skits dramatizing their solutions.

Listen to this word problem: José brought five toys to school to share. He put them on the sharing table. Hank brought three toys to share. He put them on the sharing table too. How many toys are on the sharing table?

Who wants to help me make up a skit about this word problem? (*Choose two volunteers.*) What will you use for toys? Where will you put them? What will you say? Write those things on the "Script Sheet." (*Allow time for students to demonstrate.*)

Now take your math tubs and go to your cooperative groups. I will walk around the room and help. When everyone has finished, we will meet in the large group. Each group can choose their favorite skit to present to the class.

Evaluation and Processing: Have each group tell about their experiences and discuss the process with the whole class. Ask such questions as these: What part of this activity was the most fun? The easiest? The hardest? If you did this activity again, is there anything you would do differently? Remember to use anecdotal record forms (page 18) to keep a record of participation for each student.

Script Sheet

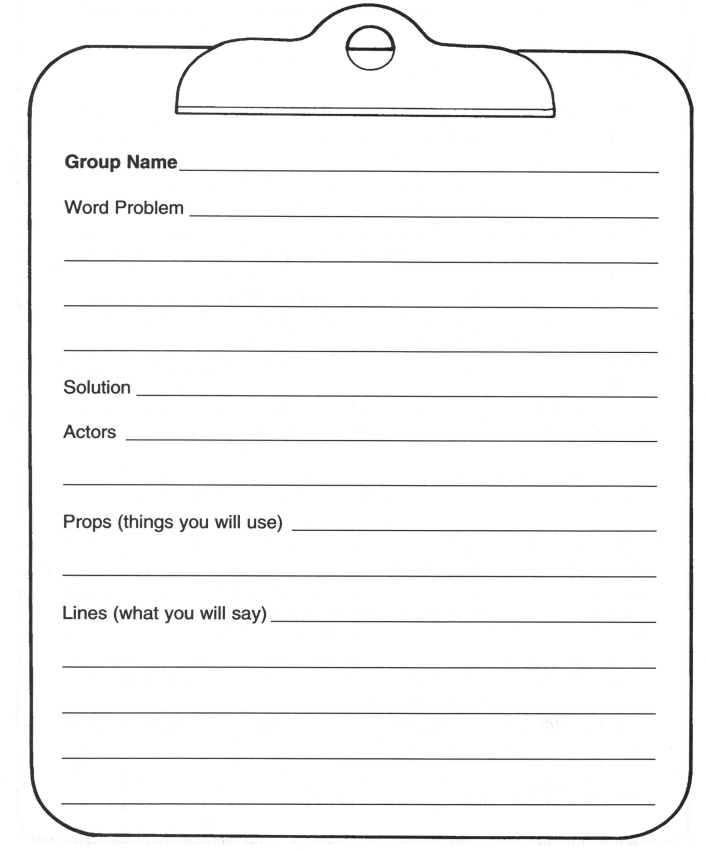

Group Name _____

Word Problem _____

_____

_____

_____

Solution _____

Actors _____

_____

Props (things you will use) _____

_____

Lines (what you will say) _____

_____

_____

_____

_____

Word Problems 1

1. The students in Mr. Lopez's room were planning a party. Vera said she could bring 36 cookies. Pham said he could bring 24 cookies. How many cookies would they have for the party?

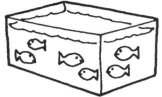 

2. The classroom aquarium was getting too crowded. Lyn took out 10 fish and left 12 fish in the aquarium. How many fish were in the aquarium to begin with?

3. The cafeteria served 80 lunches on Monday and 40 lunches on Tuesday. How many more lunches were served on Monday?

4. Ten boys got on Bus 22 and seven boys got on Bus 41. Twelve girls got on Bus 32. How many children were riding on buses?

5. Mrs. Lynch sent out 55 overdue notices from the school library last Friday. On Monday 17 of the overdue books were turned in. How many books are still overdue?

6. The 28 students in Ms. Worth's class had a big bag of candy. After each student had 2 pieces, there were still 7 pieces in the bag. How many pieces had been in the bag to begin with?

7. The children took a pet survey in their classroom. They found out that they had 17 dogs, 12 cats, 16 fish, 2 turtles, and 11 guinea pigs. How many pets did the children have all together?

8. The children took a field trip to the harbor. They saw 7 sailboats, 18 motor boats, and 2 rowboats. How many boats did they see?

Word Problems 2

1. Julie has 7 books in her desk. Nan has 6 books. Fred has 8 books. How many books do these three students have altogether?

2. Tran went to the student store to buy some supplies. He bought 3 pencils at $.10 a piece and one notebook at $1.25. How much money did Tran spend?

3. Bill lost his lunch money on the way to school. He borrowed a quarter from Liz, 50¢ from Jesse, and two dimes from Dennis. If the school lunch costs $1.00, how much more money does he need?

4. Stephanie lost two teeth last week. She plans to put them under her pillow for the Tooth Fairy. If she collects $.75 for each tooth, how much money will she have?

5. Lee picked up 77 pieces of trash on the playground. Rikki picked up 23 pieces of trash. How many pieces of trash did the students pick up altogether?

Recycle,
Reduce,
Reuse !

6. The children made 17 posters for the school poster contest. Six of the posters were about the environment. The rest were about safety. How many of the posters were about safety?

7. Mrs. Maple put two marbles in a jar every time someone in the class did something really good. At the end of the day, there were 44 marbles in the jar. How many times did Mrs. Maple see someone do something really good?

8. Ben's science book has 102 pages. His social studies book has 150 pages. How many pages do both books have altogether?

Word Problems 3

1. The students in second grade are having a food drive. Mrs. Brown's class has collected 27 cans. Mr. Evan's class has collected 14 cans. Ms. Stanhope's class has collected 25 cans. How many cans have been collected altogether?

2. Mrs. White's class is hatching chicken eggs in an incubator. They started with 20 eggs. So far, 4 baby chicks have hatched. How many eggs are still waiting to hatch?

3. There are 28 students in the classroom. When Terri started to pass out paper, she found 14 pieces on the shelf. How many more pieces does she need so that everyone will get one?

4. "We have 100 blocks and all of them are on the floor," said Mr. Cook. If the students pick up 75 blocks, how many will be left on the floor?

5. The students in Room 2 want to buy their teacher a present that costs $5.27. They have collected $3.64. How much more money will they need to collect?

6. There are 14 tables in the classroom. Two children can sit at each table. How many chairs will they need?

7. Margie bought a notebook for $1.29 and a pencil for $.15. She gave the cashier a five dollar bill. How much money did Margie get back?

8. If the children start school at 8:00 a.m. and get out at 2:30 p.m., how many hours do they spend in school?

Word Problems 4

1. Frances collects baseball cards. She has 152 cards. Bill has 98 cards. How many cards does he need to have more than Frances?

2. Dorrie walks with her mother three times a week. On Monday they walked for 25 minutes. On Wednesday they walked for 30 minutes. On Friday they walked for 20 minutes. What was the total time they spent walking during the week?

3. Fred saved his money and took his mother out to lunch. She had a hamburger that cost $.99, fries that cost $.49, and a drink that cost $.79. How much did Fred pay for his mother's lunch?

4. The students gathered up all the pencils. They found 40 pencils. Twelve of the pencils had sharp points. How many pencils needed to be sharpened?

5. The students displayed their shell collections. Meg had 25 shells and Luan had 14. How many shells were being displayed?

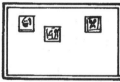

6. The students pinned 10 pictures on the front bulletin board and 15 pictures on the back bulletin board. If they had 30 pictures to begin with, how many more do they need to pin up?

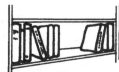

7. Mr. Williams' class got a new bookcase. They put 36 books on the first shelf, 20 books on the second shelf, and 40 books on the third shelf. How many books did they put in the bookcase?

8. Thirty children bought milk at lunch. 25 children bought orange juice. How many children bought drinks?

Word Problems 5

1. The children in the second grade had an assembly. One class needed 24 chairs. Another class needed 28 chairs. A third class needed 27 chairs. How many chairs were needed for the second grade assembly?

2. Three of the boys on the basketball team shot 20 baskets at lunchtime. Dean shot 5 of them and Glenn shot 7. How many baskets did Johnny shoot?

3. Mary collects animal erasers. She has 7 walruses, 10 dinosaurs, 2 lions, and 8 ducks. How many erasers does she have in all?

4. "We have 80 books and all of them are by the door," said Mrs. Lane. If the students check out 35 to read, how many will be left by the door?

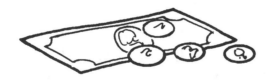

5. The students in Room 4 need $7.37 to buy a set of paints. They have collected $3.44. How much more money will they need?

6. At recess, 7 children went on the swings, 10 children went on the slide, and 9 children went on the jungle gym. How many children in all used the playground equipment?

7. One of the mothers brought a treat to the classroom. She brought 12 oranges, 9 apples, and 8 bananas. How many pieces of fruit in all did she bring?

8. Hans and Pedro are having a reading race. Hans has read 270 pages. Pedro has read 325 pages. How many pages must Hans read to catch up with Pedro?

Word Problems 6

1. David came to school with 10 marbles. He won 26 marbles at morning recess and 15 at lunch. At afternoon recess he lost 7 marbles. How many marbles does he have now?

2. Jake did 5 pull-ups, 10 sit-ups, and 12 jumping jacks. How many exercises did he do altogether?

3. The children read 20 pages during reading, 10 pages during science, and 7 more pages during social studies. How many pages did they read altogether?

4. Lots of children were sick this week. Five children had chicken pox. Six children had sore throats. Three had colds. How many children were sick?

5. The students displayed their rock collections. Randy had 41 rocks in his collection and Theresa had 25 in hers. How many rocks were being displayed?

6. Twenty-five students tried out for the school play. Nine students did not get parts. How many students did get parts?

7. Mr. Matthews made out 25 certificates to give to students who entered the science fair. Only 17 students took part. How many certificates were left over?

8. Mrs. Chan went to Europe last summer. She brought back 50 postcards to give for prizes. She has already given out 36 of them. How many does she have left?

Math in a Tub Layout

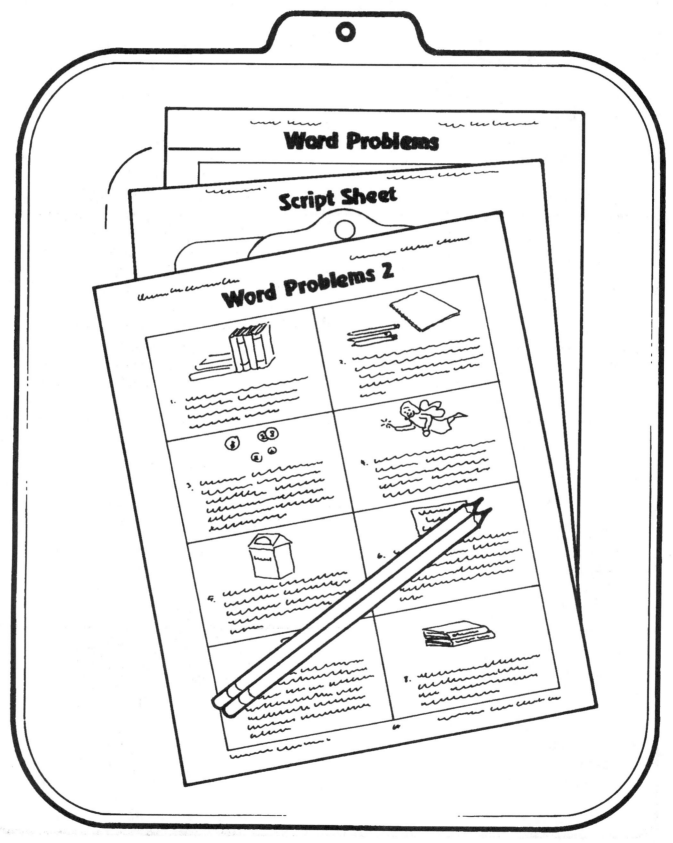

Shape Bingo

Purpose: to recognize shapes while playing a Bingo game

Skills: listening, cooperation, oral language

Mathematical Skills: visualizing, describing, and representing shapes

Materials: for each group—pencils, "Shape Bingo Activity" sheets (pages 77–78), shape playing pieces, bingo cards, container to mix up the playing pieces if desired; for whole-class activities—page 83, the materials listed on page 79

Procedure: In this activity, students learn to visualize, describe, and recognize shapes by playing Shape Bingo. To begin this activity, use the shape illustrations on page 83 to acquaint students with the various shapes. Hold a whole-class discussion in which students talk about the various shapes and how they recognize them. Ask students to name various objects around the room that are examples of the shapes. List these examples on the board. Next, have students move into their groups to complete their group activity sheets, and create the pieces for their own bingo games. (By creating the pieces for their own games, children will reinforce their understanding and knowledge about the shapes they are using.)

Next, after students have colored and cut their own game pieces, each team should have the opportunity to play their own bingo game. Some teachers may wish to divide this activity into several days as follows:

> **Day 1:** Shape discussion and team activity sheet
>
> **Day 2:** Making the game pieces and the bingo cards
>
> **Day 3:** Playing the game

Before playing Shape Bingo, model the game using the teacher script section of this activity.

To Simplify: Create the bingo game yourself to save time. Laminate and place in plastic containers or cardboard boxes and hand out with the other materials in the math tub.

To Expand: Hold a bingo tournament. Have the winners in each cooperative group meet to hold a "Winners' Bingo Game," or hold a whole-class Shape Bingo Game.

Shape Bingo *(cont.)*

Teacher Script: Today we are going to be learning about shapes. Can anyone show me a shape in our room and tell me what it is? *(Whole-class discussion about the various shapes in the room)* Now, let's look at these large shape pictures I have cut out. Let's name these shapes and talk about them. This is a square. How many sides does it have? Let's count them. One, two, three, four. Are all of the sides the same? Why don't we find out? Who has a ruler and would like to measure the sides of this square? *(Assist student volunteer in proving the sides of the square are equal in length. Model the rest of the shapes in the same manner.)*

Some examples that can be experimented with in class regarding the various other shapes are these: *rectangle* (measure sides and note opposite sides are the same length), *circle* (measure horizontally and vertically and note measurements are the same), *oval* (talk about its elongated circular shape), *triangle* (measure three sides, noting same measurements and demonstrate different kinds of triangles and different lengths of sides), and *pentagon* (measure and note same length in sides).

Now let's all move into our cooperative groups and complete our group activity sheet. Let me show you the game we are going to make. This is a Shape Bingo Game. Each of us will color the shapes on three bingo cards. Color each card exactly the same. Cut the shapes out of two of the cards. *(The shapes on the bingo cards need to match the colored and cut shapes so the game will work.)* After we have finished making our games, I will teach you how to play them. Let me know if your team needs help.

This is how we play the Shape Bingo Game. First, choose one person in your group to be the bingo "caller." A bingo caller is the person who picks the shapes and calls out their names to the rest of the group. Let's say I am the bingo caller, and the first shape I pick is this one—"blue square." Let's all look at our bingo cards. How many people have blue squares on their bingo cards? Now if you have one, take your blue square playing piece…everyone have it? *(Hold up the appropriate piece)*. Put it over the blue square on your bingo card.

What we want to do is make a line across, down, or diagonally on the bingo card. *(Model the activity.)* To get a line, we need to have heard each one of these shapes called out by the bingo caller and match the shapes to the bingo card. When you have a straight line, you yell, "Bingo!" The first person to yell "Bingo!" wins the game. Let's try this together first, and then we will play it in our cooperative groups.

Evaluation and Processing: Use the anecdotal record form on page 18 to record students' performances. Date the form before adding it to each child's portfolio. After playing the game, have students discuss their experiences. You can play this game again and again.

Shape Bingo Activity Sheet

Group Member Names:

_____

_____

1. Draw a square.

Name five things in your classroom that have a square shape.

1. _____
2. _____
3. _____
4. _____
5. _____

2. Draw a rectangle.

Name five things in your classroom that have a rectangular shape.

1. _____
2. _____
3. _____
4. _____
5. _____

3. Draw a circle.

Name five things in your classroom that have a circular shape.

1. _____
2. _____
3. _____
4. _____
5. _____

Shape Bingo Activity Sheet *(cont.)*

4. Draw an oval.

Name five things in your classroom that have an oval shape.

1. _____
2. _____
3. _____
4. _____
5. _____

5. Draw a triangle.

Name five things in your classroom that have a triangular shape.

1. _____
2. _____
3. _____
4. _____
5. _____

In the box, draw all five shapes (circle, square, triangle, oval, and rectangle) in any order. Below each shape, write its name.

Shape Bingo Game

Teacher Directions

Materials:

- "Putting the Game Together" (page 80), one for each student
- Bingo Cards (pages 81 and 82), three copies of each page for each group
- laminating material
- crayons or felt pens in yellow, blue, and red or any other three colors you choose
- scissors
- resealable plastic bag for each student
- plastic container for caller's shapes

Directions:

You may want to put the Shape Bingo Game together yourself. However, it is very easy to have students prepare the game in their cooperative groups. Here are the steps for putting your Shape Bingo Game sets together:

1. Have each student choose a different one of the card variations, A–H, and cut out all three copies of that card.

2. Have each student color each of the three cards so that they look exactly alike.

3. Laminate all of the cards when they have been colored.

4. Have each student cut up two of the cards into the individual shapes. One set of shapes will be placed in the bingo caller's container. The other set will be used by the player as game pieces. The remaining uncut card is the player's bingo card.

5. Each player can keep his or her card and corresponding game pieces in an individual resealable bag.

6. All the caller's cards can be kept in a plastic container with a lid, if desired.

7. Play and have fun!

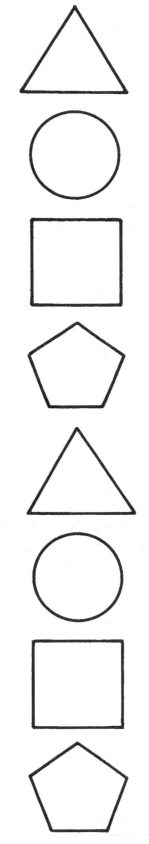

Putting the Game Together

1. Pick out your card (A-H) and cut out all three copies.

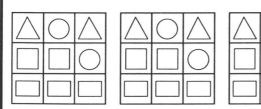

5. Cut the shapes out of two of the cards.

2. Get three crayons or markers.

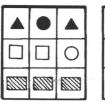

6. Save the third card.

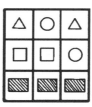

3. Color each card exactly the same.

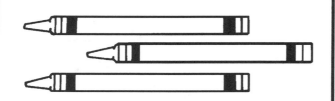

7. Put one set of shapes in a container for the caller.

4. Have your teacher help you laminate the cards.

lamin

lamin

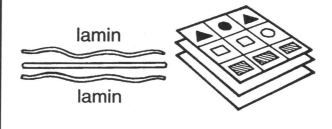

8. Put the third card in the plastic bag with the remaining shapes.

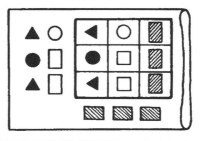

Now you are ready to play!

Bingo Cards

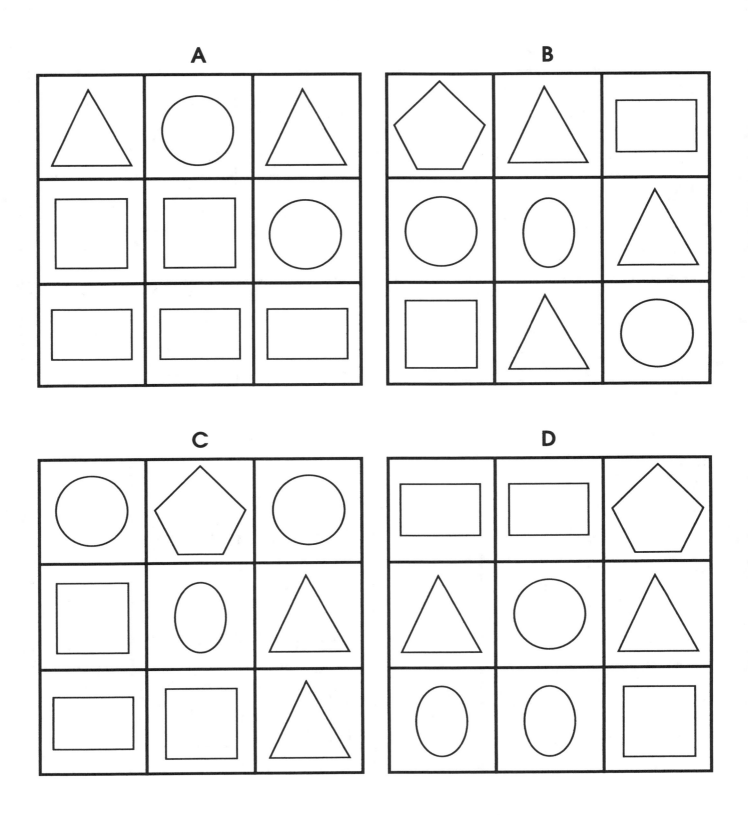

Bingo Cards *(cont.)*

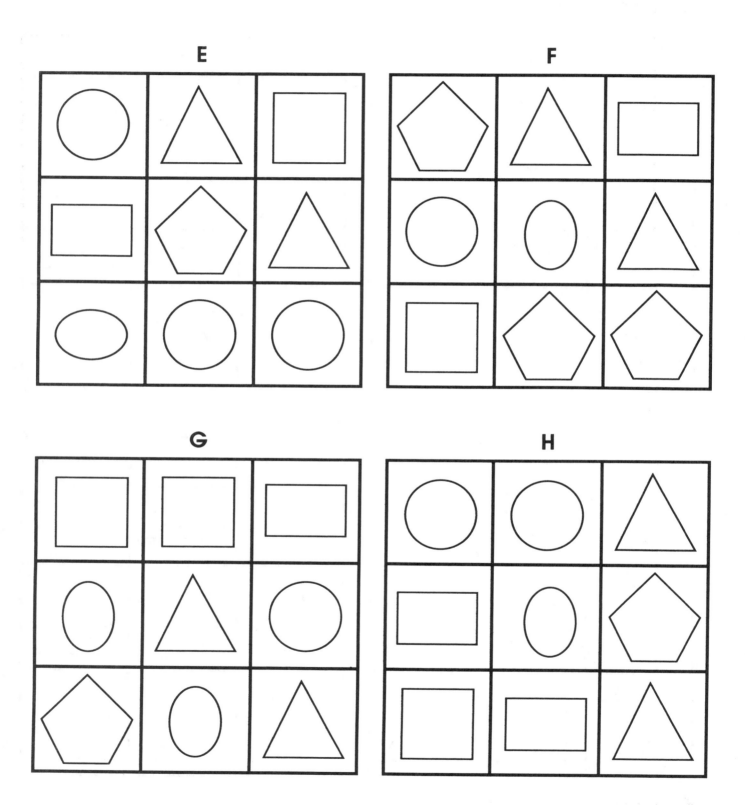

Shapes

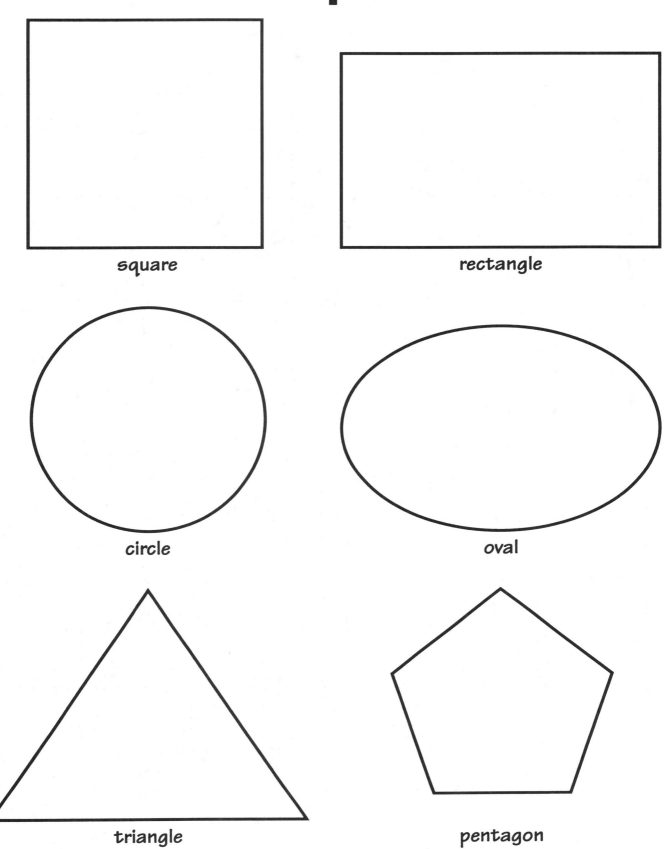

square

rectangle

circle

oval

triangle

pentagon

Math in a Tub Layout

Shape Town

Purpose: for students to use knowledge about shapes to build their own shape town

Skills: cooperating, decision making, reaching consensus, developing artistic and organizational skills

Mathematical Skills: visualizing, describing, and representing shapes

Materials: for each group—art materials, one large sheet of butcher paper for each team, bulletin board space for teams to mount their Shape Towns, a copy of page 87, scissors, glue, thumbtacks or pins, tape

Procedures: In this activity, students use their existing knowledge of shapes to create their own Shape Town. If you begin your unit about shapes by trying Shape Bingo (pages 75–84), you will probably not need to do anything else to reinforce your students' knowledge of shapes before beginning Shape Town.

To begin the activity, hold a whole-class discussion about the shapes that we see around us every day. Name a variety of example shapes that we find in our homes, our neighborhoods, our school, etc. Model the idea of a "shape town" by showing several already prepared examples of shape houses and buildings. After modeling the activity, have students meet in their cooperative groups and begin to plan their own shape towns. Meet with individual groups to hear about the plans for their towns before they begin to actually create them. This will allow you to avoid any problems and make sure each team's ideas can be done. Next, provide students with the necessary art materials and assist them in creating their towns. The finished products make wonderful Open House displays.

To Simplify: Have each group create one building. Then make a class town rather than a separate town for each group.

To Expand: Have students add to their towns by making a variety of inhabitants. It is possible to make this activity as detailed or as simple as you wish. (Shape people would be fun!)

Teacher Script: Today we are going to use what we already know about shapes to do something fun! We are going to make Shape Towns. Before we start, let's talk about the shapes in our buildings here in our own school. Let's walk around our school and see how many shapes we can find. (*Take class on a walking tour.*) Now, let's use the chalkboard to list the names of all the shapes we saw. (*Call on students for suggestions.*) We are ready now to make our shape towns. You will need to decide in your groups what kinds of buildings you would like to have in your towns.

Shape Town *(cont.)*

Teacher Script *(cont.):* Please move into your cooperative groups and decide what your towns will look like. Write your answers to the following questions on a piece of paper:

- Who will make each of the buildings?
- What extra materials would we like to have?
- Which shapes do we think we can use?

When you are ready, I will come and hear about your plans before you begin to actually make your town. When I have checked your plans, you may begin to create your buildings and mount them on your group's large sheet of butcher paper to be displayed on the bulletin board.

Evaluation and Processing: Discuss the progress of this activity with your student groups at intervals in this activity. Give students the opportunity to describe and explain their finished Shape Towns in a whole-class situation. Remember to record the students' individual participation by using the anecdotal record form on page 18.

House and Building Shapes

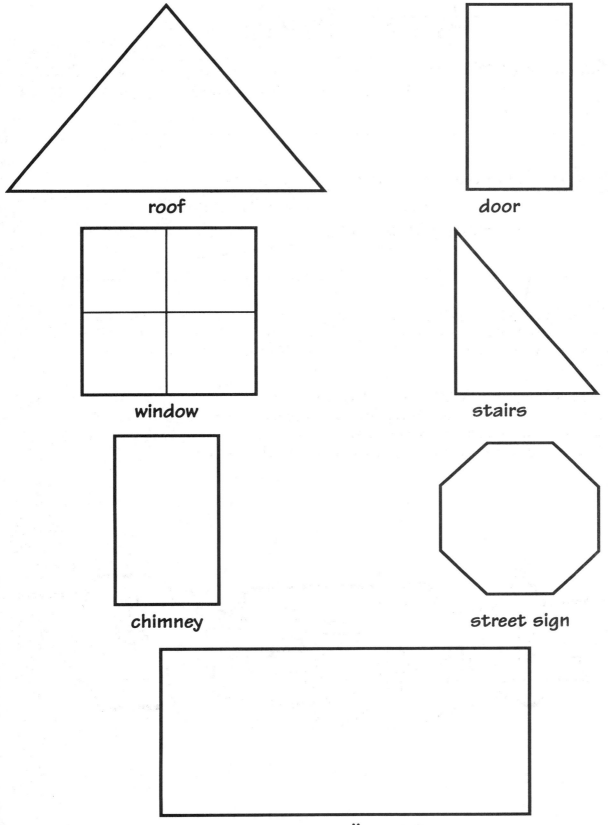

roof

door

window

stairs

chimney

street sign

wall

Math in a Tub Layout

Face Graph

Purpose: students learn how to collect data and create a visual bulletin board graph

Skills: cooperating, showing teamwork, reaching consensus, decision making, demonstrating artistic skills

Mathematical Skills: gathering and synthesizing data, making graphs

Materials: for each group—"Measurement Activity" (page 91), materials listed on page 92

Procedure: In this activity, students learn to gather data and then work together to create a face graph that compares the heights of all the students in your classroom. To begin this activity, talk with students about how we can show pictures of information or data in graphs.

Have students move into their cooperative groups and complete the "Measurement Activity" assisting each other. You will need a height chart for each student team or need to make a height chart on the bulletin board or chalkboard and have students take turns measuring themselves.

Before beginning this activity, set up the bulletin board graph. When discussing the idea of graphs and what they are used for, you will have a life-size visual model to show students how the graph will work. Begin by discussing how everyone in the classroom is a different height. Explain that graphs give us information in a way that is easy to see. *(Model the activity by showing an example face and where you would place it on the graph for yourself or a student volunteer.)*

Have students work together to determine their heights and log this information on the "Measurement Activity" page. After this, have students work in their cooperative groups to complete their own face pictures. A circle pattern is provided on page 95. As an alternative, you may wish to use a regular paper dinner plate to make the face pictures. Be sure to have a variety of art supplies available for each group so that students can be creative when making their graph faces.

To Simplify: Have students draw simple faces with crayons rather than complete art projects.

To Expand: Create a variety of different graphs using the faces again and again. Two examples could be a bar graph showing which students like one of several flavors of ice cream or a birthday graph charting students' birthdays. Students will enjoy seeing the various information pictures which they can create with the data they gather.

Face Graph *(cont.)*

Teacher Script: Today we are going to learn to make a graph. Can anyone tell me what a graph is? A graph is a picture that shows information in an easy-to-read form that explains some data that has been gathered. Today we are going to make a graph that will show us how tall everyone in our class is. It is going to go here on our bulletin board. First, though, you will have to work together in your cooperative groups to find out how tall everyone in your group is.

Use your "Measurement Activity" page to write down your answers. Everyone should move to their cooperative groups and decide what they will need to measure. After you have decided what you will need to measure your heights, come to me and ask me for the materials.

Okay, now that we have measured our heights, we are going to make our own faces to put on our graph. I am going to give paper plates to the messenger for each group. Each person in each group will draw his or her face on a paper plate. Let me show you one I did for me. We can decorate these any way we want. After we are done, we will all come back to the large group and put our classroom graph together.

Now, let's put our name tags on the bottom of the graph. After we have them on, I will call out the names, and your group spokesperson should tell me that person's height in feet and inches. We will decide together where that face should go on the graph. Good. Let's try it!

Evaluation and Processing: Let students take the faces off the graph and try it themselves in groups or in pairs to reinforce the topic. After removing the graph, place faces in individuals' portfolios. Use anecdotal record forms for additional information regarding what happened, or individual reflection forms for student feedback (pages 18 and 19).

Measurement Activity
Gathering Data

To make a face graph, each person in your group will need to find out his or her own height. What will you need to do this?

_____

Work together to find out the heights of all the students in your group. Write their height beside their names.

Name	**Height**
_____	_____
_____	_____
_____	_____
_____	_____
_____	_____

Tell your teacher your heights when you have finished listing the information. Then work together to answer these questions.

How long is a standard ruler?

_____

How many rulers does it take to equal a yardstick? (meterstick?)

_____

How many inches are in a foot? (centimeters in a meter?)

_____

How many inches are in a yard?

_____

Bulletin Board and Face Directions

Making a Face Graph Bulletin Board to Show Relative Heights

Materials:

- colored construction paper for letters
- yardstick or measuring tape
- pins, staples, or tacks
- "graph faces" prepared by students
- prepared student name tags

Procedure:

1. Select a large bulletin board space. The length of the graph will vary based on the number of students participating; the graph's height should be taller than the tallest person in the class, including teachers and aides if you would like to include them in the graph.
2. Use the Bulletin Board Idea on page 93 as a model.
3. Use the name card blanks on page 94 for students to write their names. Attach these to the board as shown on page 93.
4. Use construction paper (or commercially prepared letters and numbers) to add the heading and measuring portion to the bulletin board graph.
5. Have students decide where their own faces should go based on their heights, and attach them to the graph.

Making Graph Faces

Materials:

- paper plates, one for each student
- crayons
- paints
- markers
- yarn
- glue
- scissors

Procedure:

1. Have each student draw his or her face on either a large size dinner paper plate or a smaller dessert plate. (This will depend on the space you have available for your actual bulletin board.)
2. Provide a variety of art materials so students can add yarn-hair, skin tone, eyes, and other finishing touches.

Bulletin Board Idea

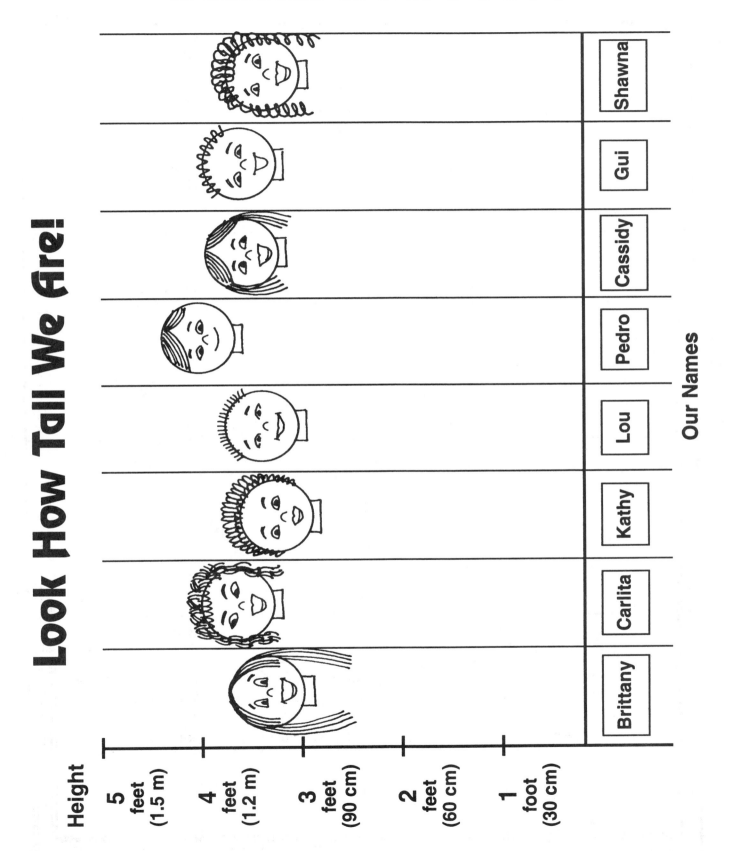

Look How Tall We Are!

Height

5 feet (1.5 m)
4 feet (1.2 m)
3 feet (90 cm)
2 feet (60 cm)
1 foot (30 cm)

Our Names

Shawna | Gui | Cassidy | Pedro | Lou | Kathy | Carlita | Brittany

Bulletin Board Name Tags

Name	Name
Name	Name
Name	Name
Name	Name

Face Graph Master

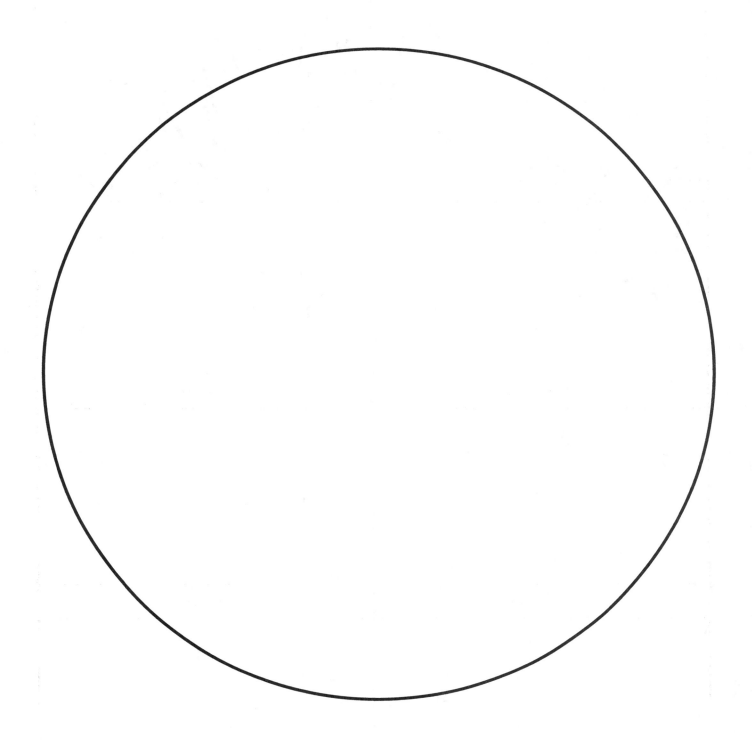

Sample Face Graph

Math in a Tub Layout

You will also need your graph faces
and a yardstick or measuring tape.

Bulletin Board Name Tags

Measurement Activity

Glue

Markers

Glue

Outdoor Graphs

Purpose: to learn the skills of data collection and graph making by creating life-sized outdoor graphs

Skills: decision making, cooperating, brainstorming, taking turns

Mathematical Skills: gathering and processing data, making and reading graphs

Materials: for each group—pages 99–101, playground chalk, outdoor black top area on which to make graphs, step ladder for aerial viewing of large graph

Procedures: Hold a whole-class discussion reviewing the Face Graph that students made. (See pages 89-97). Have students work in groups to complete the group "Data Collection Sheet" (page 99) and group graph sheets (pages 100 and 101). Next, take the class to the playground. Follow the teacher script to create the outdoor graphs. Upon completion, let students discuss the difference between seeing a life-sized picture and a small picture.

To Simplify: Forego the initial indoor step and complete a simple graph outside as a demonstration, or forego the outdoor graphs.

To Expand: Repeat this exercise a number of times, letting students decide upon ideas for graphs and ways to gather data on a variety of subjects.

Teacher Script: Today we are going to use what we have learned about gathering data and graphing to make more graphs. First, we are going to make small graphs in our cooperative groups, and then we are going to try something really different. We are going to make outdoor graphs. These outdoor graphs will be really big and interesting to look at.

Now first, let's all look again at our Face Graph on the bulletin board (page 93) and talk about how we found the data for this graph. (*Review the previous activity and its results with students.*) Now, let's all move to our cooperative groups. We are going to make a graph that will show what our favorite colors are, and then we are going to make a graph that will show when our birthdays are. Work together on your graphs and, after you get them done, we will go outside and make a life-sized outdoor graph using a small graph as our guide. If you need help, let me know.

Now, let's make a life-sized graph showing height information on the blacktop, using a yardstick and chalk. Let's fill in this graph with the data from our little graph. Great. Now let's all take turns standing on this ladder to get a bird's-eye view of this graph. Is this graph easier to read than the little graph? Which one do you like best?

Evaluation and Processing: Have students share their feelings about how this activity went. Use anecdotal record forms to chart individual performances.

Data Collection Sheet

Group Name _____

Graph One—Birthday Graph

Write the birth dates of each group member here:

Name	Month	Day
_____	_____	_____
_____	_____	_____
_____	_____	_____
_____	_____	_____
_____	_____	_____
_____	_____	_____

Now move this information to the graph called "Birthday Graph."

Graph Two—Favorite Color

Write the favorite color of each group member here:

Name	Favorite Color
_____	_____
_____	_____
_____	_____
_____	_____
_____	_____
_____	_____

Now move this information to the graph called "Favorite Colors Graph."

Favorite Colors Graph Sheet

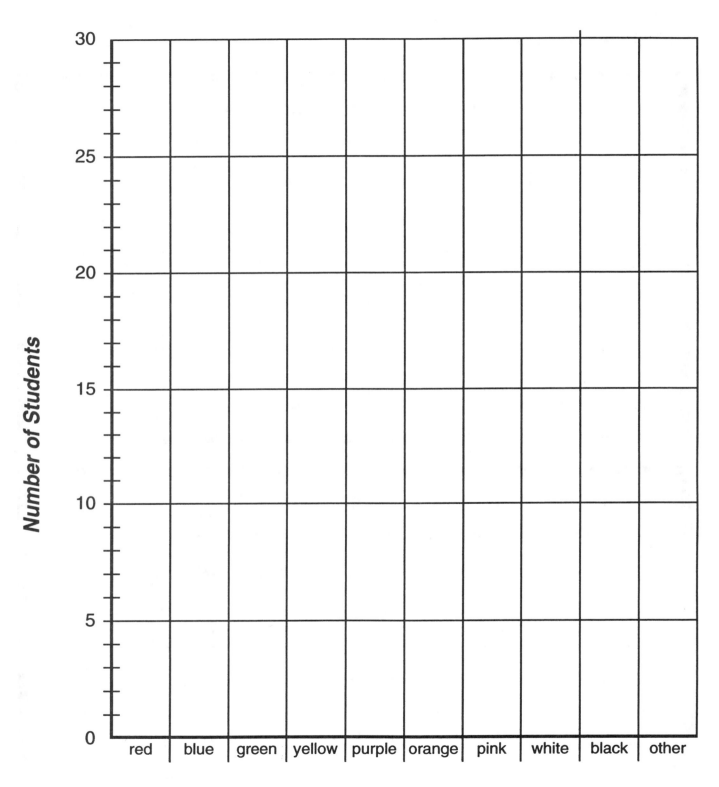

Birthday Graph Sheet

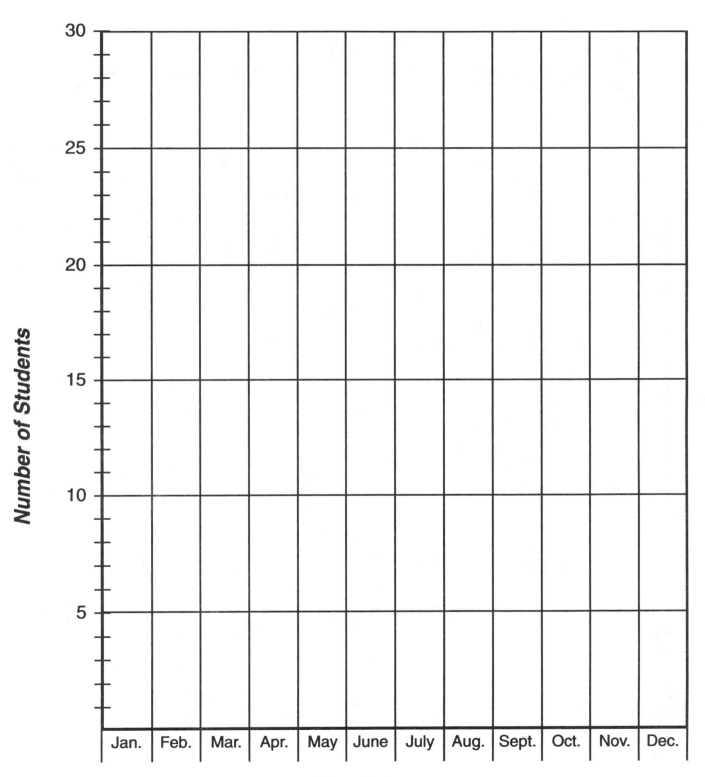

Months

Math in a Tub Layout

Treasure Hunt

Purpose: to create and use maps in a treasure hunt activity

Skills: cooperating, reaching consensus, brainstorming, and decision making

Mathematical Skills: location and mapping, estimating and planning space, creating accurate maps, interpreting maps

Materials: for each group—"Planning Sheet" (page 105), "Blank Treasure Map" (three or more copies of page 106 per group), "Sample Treasure Map" (page 107), "Treasure Chest Pattern" (page 108), treasure (different for each group— e.g., a bag of candies, certificates for free cookies from the cafeteria, etc.), shoe box or small gift box, art materials

Procedures: To begin this activity, talk about maps and their usefulness. Discuss in your whole-class group what maps are used for. Give students time to look at a variety of maps. Brainstorm the different kinds of maps and write these on the board. Next, talk about treasure maps, pirates, and hunting for treasure. Ask students to tell about movies they have seen or books they have read about pirates and buried treasure.

Have students move to their groups and plan their treasure hunt by first using their activity sheet to lead them through the process. Meet with individual groups to see whether their treasure hunt ideas are feasible. Next, provide art materials, shoe boxes, and map blanks for students to prepare their treasures, decorate their treasure chests, and hide a map in the location of their treasure. You may want to have each student group have a time alone with you in the classroom to hide their treasure to make the suspense more fun for student teams. Have each student group pick another group's name out of a hat or assign names so two teams can work together to find a treasure by using a map. You may wish to have this activity take place over a week, ending in a pirate party! (See page 104 for daily activities.)

To Simplify: Use any of these steps, but not all, to make an easier activity.

To Expand: Have students research pirates and treasure and learn something about the historical background of treasures and treasure maps.

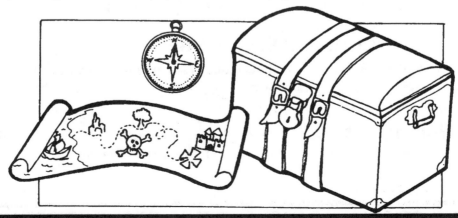

Treasure Hunt *(cont.)*

Teacher Script:

Day 1—Map Ideas and Planning

Today we are going to talk about maps. Let's look at these examples I have of maps. *(Show examples of available maps: world, state, county, city and smaller areas, as well as globes.)* This week, we are going to pretend we are pirates and make and hide a secret treasure! Each group will make a map and let another group find its treasure. To begin, who can tell us about a movie or a book that is about pirates and treasure? *(Encourage enough plot sharing to set the scene for having a treasure hunt.)* Now that we are all thinking about pirates and treasure, we will go to our groups and work together using our group "Planning Sheet" to plan our own treasure hunt. After you decide what you want to do about your treasure, I will talk to each group about your decisions.

Day 2—Creating Treasure Chests

Yesterday you made some decisions in your groups. Today you are going to make your treasure chests. Use your "Treasure Chest Pattern," your shoe box, and art materials to decorate it. I will walk around and help anyone who needs help.

Day 3—Planning and Drawing Maps

Look at your planning sheet and use the clues you decided on to plan your map. Then draw the map in such a way that it will help another team find your treasure. It should be clear but not too easy. You might want to use "pirate words" and symbols on your map. Sketch it in pencil and ask me to check it before you use crayons or markers.

Day 4—Finishing Maps and Hiding Treasure

Today you may finish your maps if you did not finish yesterday. I will help each group to hide its treasure. I will give you each a special time. *(Meet with one group at recess, and another at the beginning of lunch. You might keep another group in a few minutes when the rest go out to P.E. or at the end of the day.)*

Day 5—Treasure Hunt and Pirate Party

Today we will exchange maps and have our treasure hunt. When everyone has found a treasure, we will have a Pirate Party to celebrate. *(Serve simple refreshments and discuss the activity.)*

Evaluation and Processing: Ask students what they liked best about the
activity. What was hardest? Easiest? What would they do differently if they did it again?

Planning Sheet

Group Name _____

What will you call your band of pirates? Use the back of this
page to design your flag.

_____

Where will you hide your treasure?

_____

_____

What clues will you give on your map?

_____

_____

What is your second choice for a hiding place?

_____

_____

What clues will you give on your map?

_____

_____

Blank Treasure Map

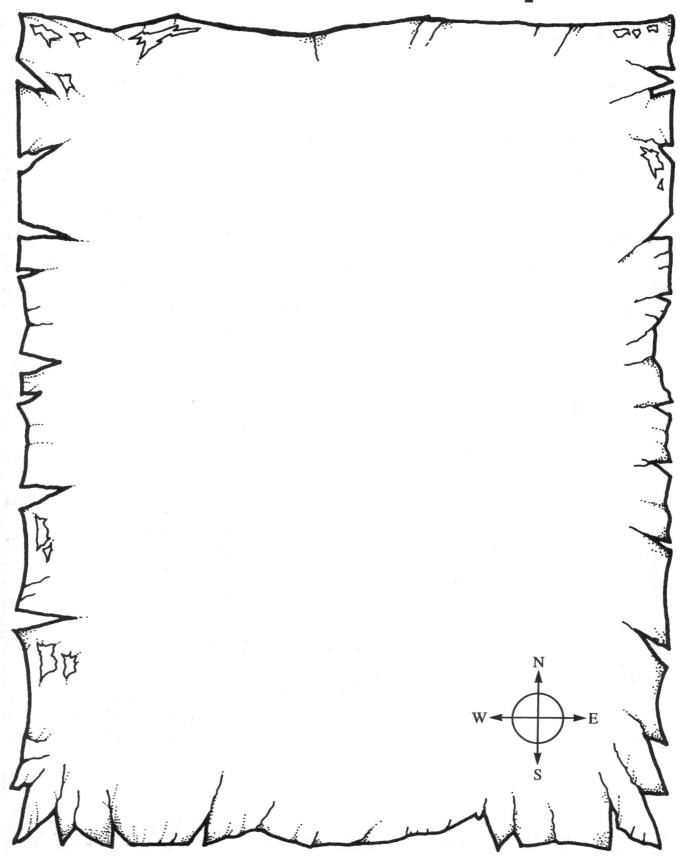

Sample Treasure Map

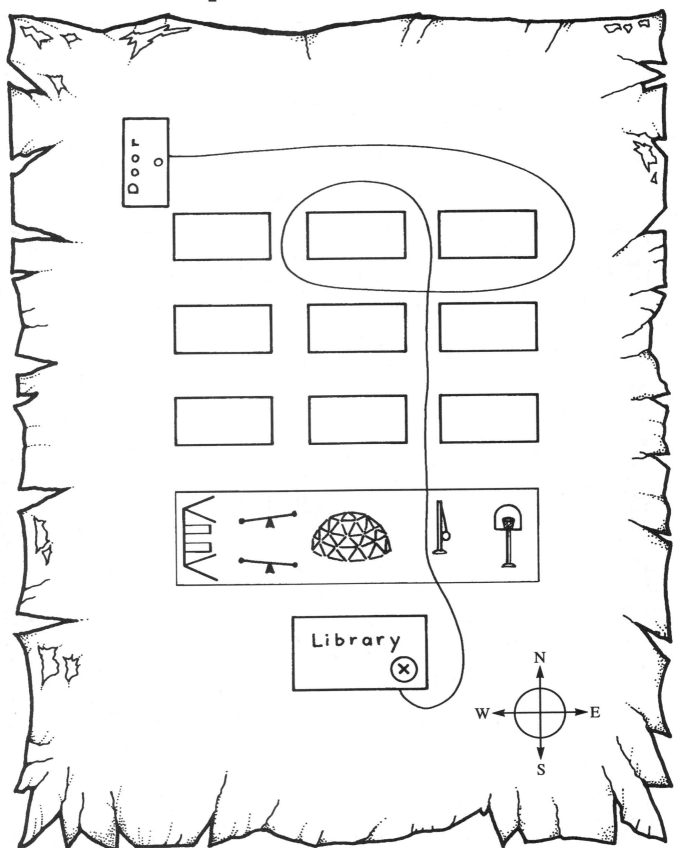

Treasure Chest Pattern

Use crayons to decorate your treasure chest. Cut it out and paste it to the front of a box.

Math in a Tub Layout

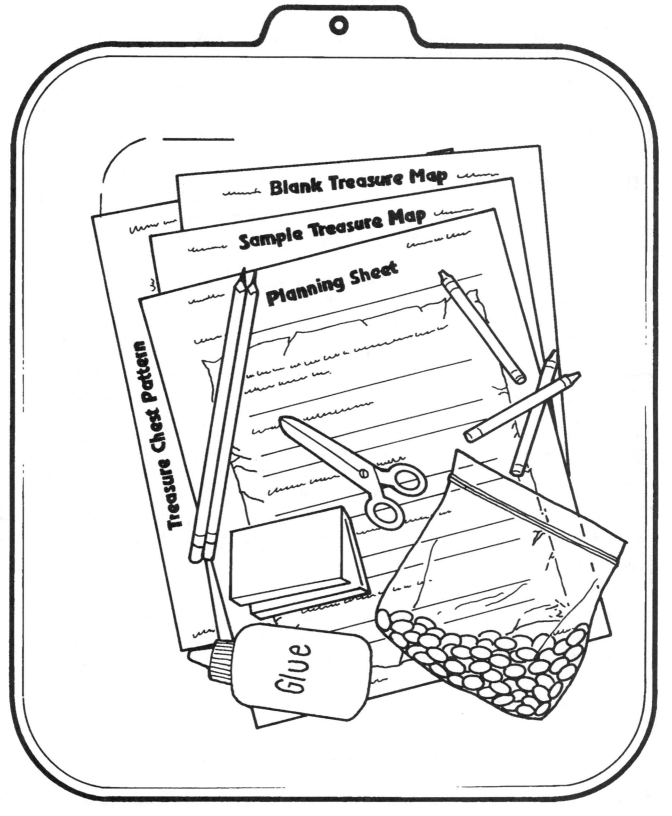

Weighing Things

Purpose: to learn the concept and process of balancing weights as an experimental approach to weighing objects

Skills: following directions, cooperating, using oral and written language skills, using coordination skills

Mathematical Skills: estimating, verifying, using a balance scale, recording data

Materials: for each group—one balance scale per group (simple plastic balance scales are fine), weights for scale, an accumulation of small objects to weigh, including a one-foot ruler and some unsharpened pencils (at least some of the objects should be different for each group), copies of pages 112 and 113 (Make some extra copies to allow for mistakes.), sharpened pencils

Procedures: With the whole class, discuss and demonstrate the use of a simple balance scale: balance identical weights, equivalent weights, and weights of small objects. Before weighing each object, ask students to guess how many weights will need to be placed on the other side of the scale. Tell students that they will have time in their cooperative groups to experiment with and practice these skills. Model the use of the "Guess, Weigh, and Record 1."

After the whole-class demonstration, have students work in their cooperative groups. Encourage them to spend enough time for each person in the group to become familiar with the use of the scale and weights. Before they begin to weigh objects, have students decide how to share the tasks. It works well to have them choose someone to make an estimate, someone to actually weigh an object, and someone to record the data. These jobs can rotate around the group so everyone has a chance to play each role.

Have students continue the activity by guessing which objects will balance each other and then testing their guesses. (One ruler might balance ten paper clips, for example.) This data should be recorded on page 113.

Have students save the "Guess, Weigh, and Record" activity sheets for the next activity.

To Simplify: Have students work with an older student or parent helper who will help them discuss and record their findings as they go along.

To Expand: Have each student write a series of directions for weighing something using a balance scale. Then have each student exchange directions with another student and follow the directions exactly. Students can watch each other and make necessary corrections to improve their directions.

Weighing Things *(cont.)*

Teacher Script: Today you are going to work in groups to learn how to weigh objects using a simple balance scale. First, I am going to show you how to weigh things on a balance scale. *(Display scale.)* If I put one weight on this side of the scale, it will go down. If I add weight to the other side of the scale, that side will go down. If the weights are equal, the two sides will balance and this pointer will be in the center. *(Demonstrate.)* The weights don't have to be exactly the same. For example, these two small weights balance this larger one. We can also weigh small objects this way. How much do you think this toy truck will weigh? *(Call on several students.)* Let's try it. This toy truck needs two of the larger weights to balance it, so it weighs____.

You will have time in your cooperative groups to experiment with and practice these skills. When you have all had a chance to use the scale, you will choose people to start guessing, weighing, and writing down your findings. The jobs will move around the group, so everyone gets a chance to do it all. *(Model the way the jobs will move and the use of the "Guess, Weigh, and Record" activity sheet).*

When you are in your cooperative groups, please take enough time for each person in your group to use the scale. Raise your hands when your group is ready to go on. Then choose the three people who will start. The first person will pick an object and guess its weight. The second person will actually weigh the object. The third person will record both the guess and the actual weight on the activity sheet. Please take your math tubs and move to your cooperative groups.

After you finish the first activity sheet, you can continue the activity by guessing which objects will balance each other and then testing your ideas. One ruler might balance ten paper clips, for example. Use the second activity sheet to write down this information.

When you finish both activity sheets, write your group's name on them and give them to me to save for the next activity we will do.

Evaluation and Processing: Have each group tell about their experiences and discuss the process with the whole class. Ask such questions as these: Which role did you enjoy the most? Did it get easier to guess the weight of an object as you went along? Were you surprised at any of your results? Can anybody guess what we are going to do with the information we gathered? *(Write the guesses on the board and save to compare with the actual activity that follows.)* Remember to use anecdotal record forms (page 18) to keep a record of students' participation.

Guess, Weigh, and Record 1

Group Name_____ Date _____

Object	Guess	Actual Weight
_____	_____	_____
_____	_____	_____
_____	_____	_____
_____	_____	_____
_____	_____	_____
_____	_____	_____
_____	_____	_____
_____	_____	_____
_____	_____	_____
_____	_____	_____
_____	_____	_____
_____	_____	_____
_____	_____	_____
_____	_____	_____

Guess, Weigh, and Record 2

Group Name_____ Date _____

Objects	Equivalent Objects

Math in a Tub Layout

Balancing Act

Purpose: to use the concept of weight to make a mobile

Skills: following directions, cooperation, coordination, artistic skills

Mathematical Skills: estimating, verifying, using previous knowledge to balance objects

Materials: for each group—one mobile hanger, the same small objects that were weighed in the previous activity (Groups should have the tubs they worked with before.), one additional ruler, pipe cleaners, heavy black thread or nylon fishing line, scissors

Procedures: Student groups construct mobiles using the small objects in their tubs and the data from the previous activity. Discuss/demonstrate how to begin making a mobile. (Prepare a mobile in advance for demonstration. See "Directions for Making a Mobile" on pages 116 and 117.) Show students how to use the information they recorded on their "Guess, Weigh, and Record" activity sheets.

After the whole-class demonstration, have students take their math tubs and completed worksheets to their groups. Allow plenty of time for students to use a trial-and-error approach to construct their mobiles. Make yourself available to assist the groups.

Finally, have students present and explain their mobiles to the whole class.

To Simplify: Have students make very simple mobiles using a limited, specified number of objects.

To Expand: Have students attempt to use all the objects in their tubs.

Teacher Script: Let's look at the guesses people made about today's activity. *(Review guesses that were written on the board.)* Today we are going to make mobiles. Was anyone right? Mobiles are objects that hang and move in the air because they are balanced. You already know a lot about balancing the things you are going to use because you wrote down what you did in the last activity.

(Demonstrate each step.) Here is a simple mobile that I made. Start by tying a piece of heavy black thread (or fishing line) to the middle of one of your one-foot rulers. Make a loop in the other end of your thread. Hang the ruler from your group's hook.

Next, look at your completed activity on page 113. Find some objects that balance. *(Continue to demonstrate, substituting the names of the objects you use.)* I know that this yo-yo weighs the same as these two toy cars. I will use pipe cleaners to hang the yo-yo from one end of the ruler and the two cars from the other end. I can push them back and forth a little until they balance perfectly. I can also be much fancier and hang two more rulers or two pencils from the end of the first ruler, and go on from there. Be as creative as you want. If the first thing you try doesn't work, try something else. Now take your tubs and go to your groups. When all the mobiles are finished, we will share with the whole class.

Evaluation and Processing: Have each group present and explain their mobiles.

Directions for Making a Mobile

Mobile hangers:

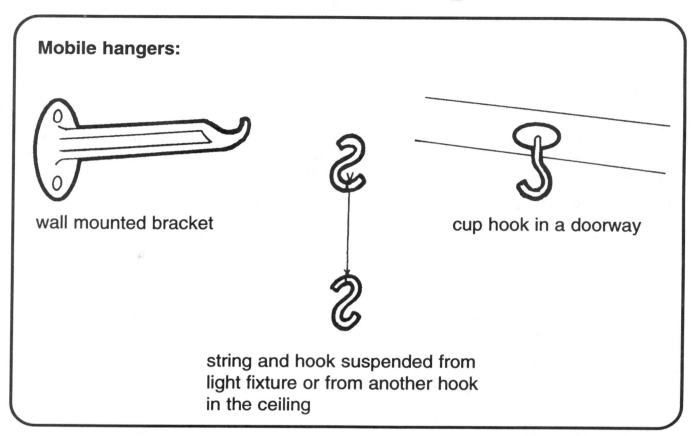

wall mounted bracket

cup hook in a doorway

string and hook suspended from
light fixture or from another hook
in the ceiling

Using pipe cleaners:

Directions for Making a Mobile *(cont.)*

Simple mobile:

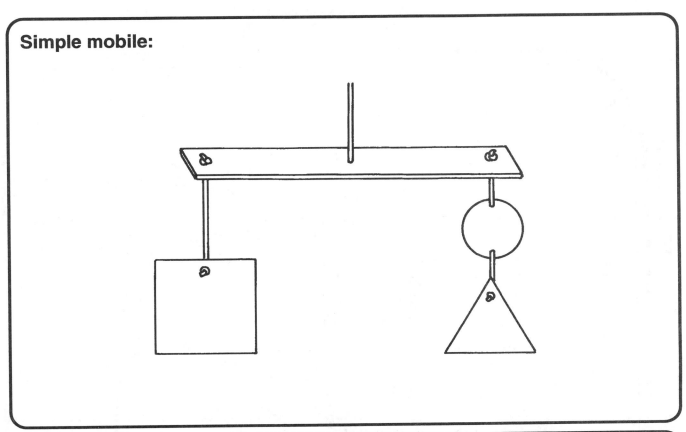

Complex mobile:

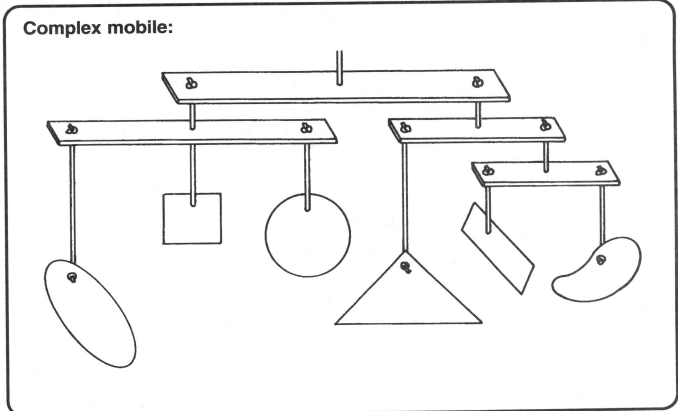

Math in a Tub Layout

The labels visible on the pages in the tub read:
- Guess, Weigh, and Record 2
- Guess, Weigh, and Record 1
- Directions for Making a Mobile (cont.)
- Directions for Making a Mobile

Find the Shapes

Purpose: to review a variety of shapes, their names, and characteristics in preparation for learning to measure these shapes

Skills: following directions, cooperation, oral and written language skills

Mathematical Skills: shape recognition, measurement of shapes using a non-standard unit of measurement

Special Note: Prepare for this activity by enlisting the help of other teachers who will agree to have your students come to their classrooms to ask for items for their scavenger hunt. Go over the kind of good manners you expect from your scavenger hunters; have them write the names of the participating teachers and the room numbers on their "Check-Off Sheets" before leaving your classroom.

Materials: page 121 (one for each student plus extras), one of the same kind plus extras of pages 123–128 for each group member (Give different lists to each group. This will allow for more success, since the teachers will soon run out of selected items.), large paper grocery bags (one for each student), pencils, 6–8 large metal paper clips per group

Procedures: Students review shapes and shape names and then work in groups to organize a scavenger hunt. They will collect objects that match the shapes on their "Check-Off Sheets." Students will measure selected items using paper clips.

With the whole class, first review the names and characteristics of the shapes listed on page 121. Ask students to describe shapes and copy onto page 121 the drawings you make on the board (see "Teacher's Reference Sheet" on page 122). Then familiarize them with the idea of a scavenger hunt. Write on the board the names and room numbers of the participating teachers; students copy them on their "Check-Off Sheets." Review expected behavior with students. Have students work in groups to organize and carry out a scavenger hunt. When all students have returned from the scavenger hunt, have them use paper clips to measure either the length of a side of their item or the length of one edge of their cube and write this measurement in the appropriate place on their "Check-Off Sheets." Have members of each group present some items to the whole class. Compare measurements and observe the items that were measured. A prize can be given to members of the winning group, or certificates can be given to all (see page 129).

To Simplify: Have students suggest items to find for each shape (chalk, eraser, ball, etc.) as part of the large-group discussion.

To Expand: Have groups look up and write characteristics of each shape on page 121 instead of being given this information in the large-group discussion.

Find the Shapes (cont.)

Teacher Script: Today we are going to talk about shapes. *(Pass out Page 121.)* Look at the names of shapes on this page. The first one is rectangle. Who can tell me what makes a rectangle different from other shapes? Right. A rectangle has four sides. The sides directly across from each other are exactly the same length. It has four corners that are right angles. Use your hands to show me what a right angle looks like. *(Write rectangle on chalk board and sketch the shape.)* Draw a small rectangle like mine next to the word rectangle on your "Shapes Activity Sheet." The next shape is square. A square is a special kind of rectangle. Who can tell me what makes it special? *(Continue in this manner through the shape names. See "Teacher's Reference Sheet" on page 122.)*

Now, who can tell us what a scavenger hunt is? *(Listen to students' explanations and clarify as may be necessary.)* We will all be going on a scavenger hunt today. Some teachers have agreed to help us. These are the names and room numbers of those teachers. *(Write this information on the board.)* Please copy them on to the "Check-Off Sheets" that are in your math tubs before you leave the room. *(Review with students the behavior you expect when they go to another classroom. Then have them take their tubs and go to their groups to get organized for the scavenger hunt.)*

When you have all returned from your scavenger hunts, use paper clips to measure one side of your square object or one edge of your cube object. Write this information on your "Check-Off Sheet." Then we will look at and discuss everyone's shapes.

Evaluation and Processing: Have each group tell about their experiences and discuss the process with the whole class. Ask such questions as these: Which shape was hardest to find? Which was easiest? Did you decide ahead of time what to ask for? Remember to use anecdotal record forms (page 18) to keep a record of each child's participation in the activity.

Shapes Activity Sheet

rectangle	octagon	pyramid
square	parallelogram (diamond)	cone
triangle	ellipse (oval)	cylinder
circle	cube	sphere
pentagon	rectangular prism	ellipsoid (egg)

Teacher's Reference Sheet

Rectangle: a four-sided plane figure with four right angles

Square: a rectangle with four equal sides

Triangle: a plane figure with three angles and three sides

Circle: a plane figure made up of a curved line; every point on the line is the same distance from the center of the figure

Pentagon: a plane figure with five angles and five sides

Octagon: a plane figure with eight angles and eight sides

Parallelogram: a four-sided plane figure that has two sets of parallel lines. A diamond is a parallelogram younger students can recognize.

Ellipse (oval): a plane figure shaped like an egg

Cube: a solid figure with six equal, square sides

Rectangular prism: a solid figure with right-angled corners and six sides

Pyramid: a solid figure with triangular or rectangular base and triangular sides that meet in a point at the top

Cone: a solid figure with a circle as a base and a curved surface tapering to a point

Cylinder: a solid figure shaped like a can with a curved surface and a circle on each end

Sphere: a solid figure shaped like a ball

Ellipsoid (egg): a solid figure shaped like an egg

Check-Off Sheet 1

Group Name _____   Student Name _____

Classrooms Taking Part

_____   _____   _____

_____   _____   _____

_____   _____   _____

List of Things to Find

Shape	Item	Return to
circle		
pentagon		
triangle		
cube		
square		
cone		
cylinder		
sphere		

length of one side of square= _____ paper clips

Check-Off Sheet 2

Group Name _____   Student Name _____

Classrooms Taking Part

_____   _____   _____

_____   _____   _____

_____   _____   _____

List of Things to Find

Shape	Item	Return to
ellipsoid (egg)		
square		
pyramid		
triangle		
cube		
sphere		
cylinder		
octagon		

length of one edge of cube= _____ paper clips

Check-Off Sheet 3

Group Name _____   Student Name _____

Classrooms Taking Part

_____   _____   _____

_____   _____   _____

_____   _____   _____

List of Things to Find

Shape	Item	Return to
rectangle		
cone		
octagon		
sphere		
pyramid		
cylinder		
cube		
triangle		

length of one edge of cube= _____ paper clips

Check-Off Sheet 4

Group Name _____ Student Name _____

Classrooms Taking Part

_____   _____   _____

_____   _____   _____

_____   _____   _____

List of Things to Find

Shape	Item	Return to
ellipse (oval)		
cylinder		
square		
cube		
pyramid		
cone		
octagon		
sphere		

length of one side of square= _____ paper clips

Check-Off Sheet 5

Group Name _____ Student Name _____

Classrooms Taking Part

_____ _____ _____

_____ _____ _____

_____ _____ _____

List of Things to Find

Shape	Item	Return to
rectangular prism		
sphere		
cone		
pyramid		
square		
triangle		
pentagon		
octagon		

length of one side of square= _____ paper clips

Check-Off Sheet 6

Group Name _____ Student Name _____

Classrooms Taking Part

_____   _____   _____

_____   _____   _____

_____   _____   _____

List of Things to Find

Shape	Item	Return to
diamond		
cube		
octagon		
triangle		
pyramid		
pentagon		
cylinder		
cone		

length of one edge of cube= _____ paper clips

Scavenger Hunt Certificate

_____

has successfully completed a Shapes Scavenger Hunt

• • • • • • • • • • • • • •

and knows the names and characteristics of these shapes:

square	octagon	pyramid
rectangle	diamond	cone
triangle	ellipse (oval)	cylinder
circle	cube	sphere
pentagon	rectangular prism	ellipsoid (egg)

_____   _____
            Teacher   *Date*

Math in a Tub Layout

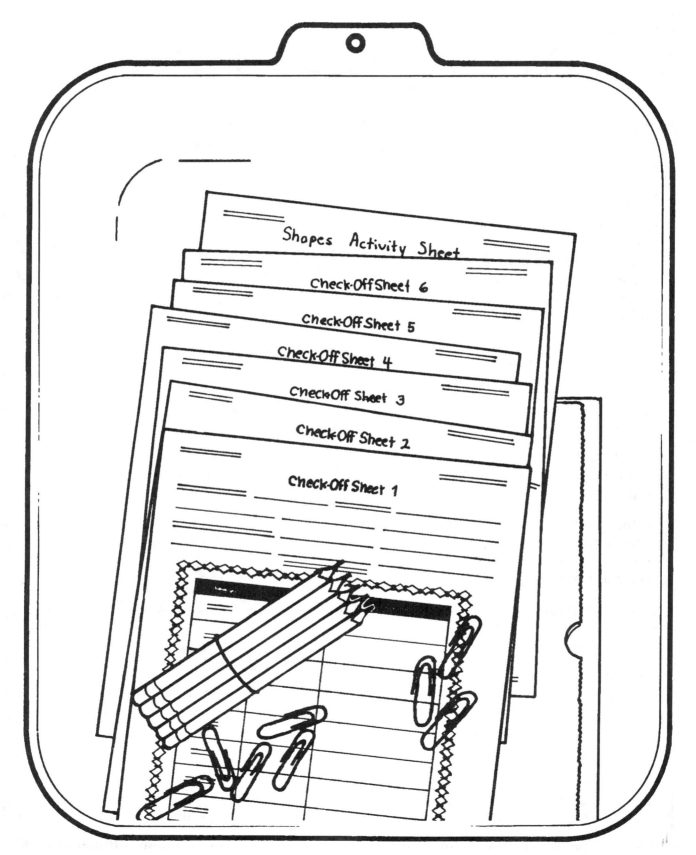

Shapes Activity Sheet

Check-Off Sheet 6

Check-Off Sheet 5

Check-Off Sheet 4

Check-Off Sheet 3

Check-Off Sheet 2

Check-Off Sheet 1

Why Aren't They the Same?

Purpose: to compare nonstandard measurements of the same lengths

Skills: following directions, cooperation

Mathematical Skills: measuring, tallying, counting by 5s, drawing conclusions

Materials: one "Tally Sheet" for each student plus extras; objects to use for nonstandard units of measure, some large and some small, different for each group (paper clips, unsharpened pencils, chalkboard erasers, blocks, textbooks, chalk, playing cards); pencils

Procedures: First, use the Teacher Script to review linear measurement techniques, to show students how to tally, and to demonstrate the cooperative group activities. Ask students to assign someone to kneel down and move the unit of measurement, someone to mark the place, someone to count the measurement, and someone to make the tally marks. Then have them count up their tally marks and record the lengths they measured. Finally, meet in a whole-group and compare measurements. Have students draw conclusions about why the measurements are not the same. Discuss the advantages of having standard units of measurement.

To Simplify: Have students measure a smaller object, such as a table top.

To Expand: Have groups measure more than one thing—the width of the room in addition to the length, the length of the playground slide, the distance to the lunchroom or cafeteria, etc.

Teacher Script: Today you will all be using different nonstandard units of measurement to measure the same thing—the length of the classroom. We will then compare results.

First, let's make sure you will all be using the same measuring technique. Who wants to demonstrate? Okay, Jill. Use this piece of paper to demonstrate. Place the end against the wall. Mark the place where the paper ends. Then move the paper and start again at the mark you made.

Now, let's make sure everyone knows how to tally by making four straight lines (||||) and a slash (/) to keep track of 5s on your tally sheet. Tally marks are easy to count by 5s. Let's all count to 100 by 5s.

Decide who will do each job when you get to your group. You need someone to kneel down and move the unit of measurement, someone to mark the place, someone to count the measurements, and someone to make the tally marks. If you have people left over, they can double-check the measuring and tallying. When we have finished, we will compare results.

Evaluation and Processing: Have groups share their processes with the whole class. Ask such questions as these: Which unit of measurement did your group use? What was your result? Why are all the measurements different? What are the advantages of having standard units of measurement? Remember to use anecdotal record forms.

Group Name _____

Tally Sheet

Jobs/Students

_____

_____

_____

Nonstandard Unit of Measurement _____

Tally Marks

Total Length _____

Math in a Tub Layout

Tally Sheet

CHALKBOARD Eraser

Shape-Trading Designs

Purpose: to explore the equivalence of shapes through the construction of geometric designs

Skills: following directions, cooperation, creativity

Mathematical Skills: spatial visualization, exchanging shapes with their equivalents

Materials: for each group—pages 136 and 137 for each person in the group, large sheets of construction paper, pencils, scissors, glue sticks, construction paper scraps in a variety of colors

(You may choose to precut multiple sets of shapes from construction paper in a variety of colors.)

Procedures: Students work in groups, but construct individual geometric designs, beginning with the large rectangle shape. They then trade all large rectangles for their equivalents in other shapes until they have replaced them all and are pleased with the designs they have created.

First, go over the directions sheet with the students, making your own design with large rectangles and then trading them for equivalent shapes. Demonstrate using a tiny dab of glue to hold the shapes down temporarily.

Next, have students take their math tubs and move to their groups. They should choose someone to begin and take turns as they follow their direction sheets. Make yourself available to assist students.

Finally, have students share their completed designs with the class.

To Simplify: Supply only one or two shapes in addition to the large rectangles and follow the regular procedure.

To Expand: Allow students to make their designs more elaborate by cutting in half the small triangle, the square, and the small rectangle.

Teacher Script: Today you will work in your groups to construct individual geometric designs, using these shapes. *(Show shapes.)* You will start by making designs using just the large rectangle. Then you will trade all the large rectangles for their equivalents in other shapes. Equivalent shapes cover the same area. Let me show you. Two squares take up the same space as the large rectangle. Two small rectangles take up the same space as the square. *(Demonstrate, using shapes.)*

Shape-Trading Designs *(cont.)*

Teacher Script *(cont.)*: *(Pass out directions sheets.)* Look at your directions sheets as I demonstrate.

First I will choose a large piece of construction paper. I like red, so I will choose red. I can place it either this way *(vertically)* or this way *(horizontally)*.

Next, I will trace the pattern for the large rectangle on these small pieces of construction paper and cut them out.

Then I will place the rectangles in a design on the large piece of construction paper and move them around until I have a design I like. Watch me as I put a tiny dab of glue on the back of each rectangle so they won't move around if I bump my design or sneeze!

Now I will take the other shape patterns and cut out many squares, small rectangles, and large and small triangles. I will use many different colors. When I am finished, I will put them in the center of the table.

The next step will be for you to choose someone in your group to be first. That person will trade one of his or her large rectangles for shapes that are equivalent and put them in the same place on the large design. I will trade this rectangle for two large triangles. When I have my next turn, I might trade a rectangle for two squares or four small triangles. Remember to use a tiny dab of glue to keep them from moving around.

I will keep doing this until all the large rectangles have been replaced with other shapes and I am happy with my design. I can also trade other shapes, as long as the ones I trade for cover the same area. If you run out of shapes you need, you may cut more or trade with each other. When you finish your design, glue the pieces down permanently. Be ready to share your design with the class.

Now, take your math tubs and move to your groups. Choose someone to begin and take turns as you follow your directions sheets. I will walk around and help.

Evaluation and Processing: Have each group share with the whole class.
Ask such questions as these: How did you decide who would be first? What shapes did you trade for first? How many times did you trade? What colors did you use? Were colors important to you as you made your design? Use anecdotal record forms (page 18) to keep a record of participation for each student.

Directions for Shape-Trading Designs

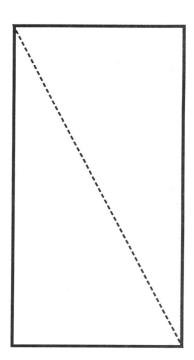

1. Choose a large piece of construction paper in a color you like. Put it on the table in front of you. It can be either up-and-down (vertical) or sideways (horizontal).

2. Cut out the large rectangle. Trace it 4–6 times on a different colored construction paper. Cut them out. You can cut more as you decide you need them.

3. Place the rectangles in a design on the large piece of construction paper. Move them around until you have a design you like. Trace and cut more if you want. Put a tiny dab of glue on the back of each rectangle, so they won't move around if you bump your design (or sneeze!).

4. Now, trace and cut out some squares, small rectangles, and some large and small triangles. Use lots of different colors. Put the shapes you cut out in the center of the table.

5. Choose someone in your group to be first. That person will trade one of his or her large rectangles for shapes that are equivalent (cover the same area) and put them in the same place on the large design. Remember to use a tiny dab of glue.

6. Take turns, going around and around the table, until all of the large rectangles have been replaced with other shapes and everyone is satisfied with his or her design. (You can also trade other shapes, as long as the ones you trade for cover the same area.) If you run out of the shapes you need in the pile in the middle of the table, you may cut more or trade with each other.

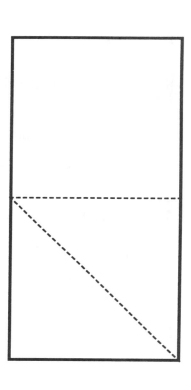

7. When you finish your design, glue the pieces down permanently.

8. Be ready to display and talk about your design with the class.

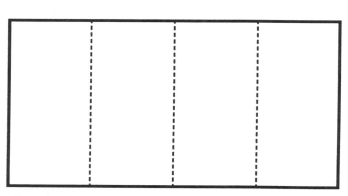

Shape Patterns

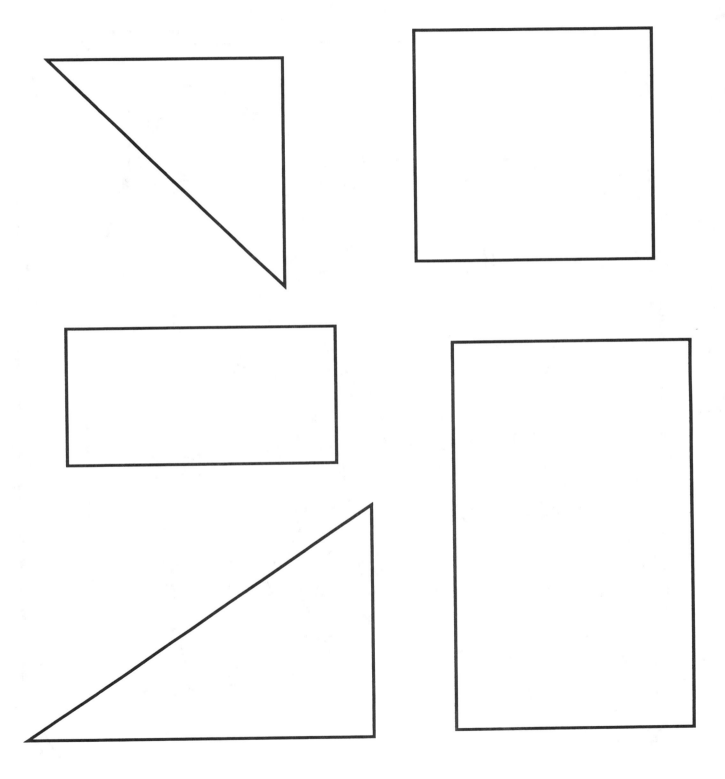

Math in a Tub Layout

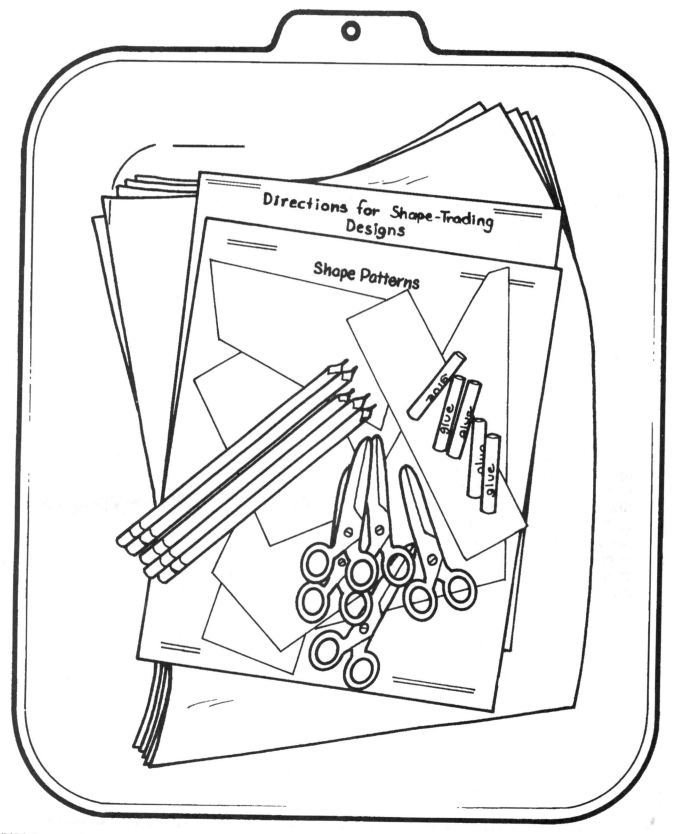

Directions for Shape-Trading Designs

Shape Patterns

glue

glue

glue

glue

Value Charts

Purpose: to explore the variety of coin combinations that can represent a given value

Skills: following directions, cooperating, using creativity, using oral language skills

Mathematical Skills: knowledge of the value of all U.S. coins in relation to the dollar, ability to compare money values, ability to create new combinations to arrive at a fixed value

Materials: for each group—copies of pages 141–143 (Have extra coins cut from page 143 available for groups.), small resealable plastic bags for paper coins; for the class chart—butcher paper, scissors, markers, rulers or yardsticks (to be used as straightedges for drawing chart lines on butcher paper)

Procedures: Students work in their groups to find a variety of coin combinations that, when added, equal a half-dollar.

Cut out coins from page 143. (It is not necessary to make cuts around the coin edges. Simply cut a strip of coins and then cut in between each coin on the strip.) Place sets of coins in plastic bags and then in tubs along with pages 141 and 142. Prepare a large "Coin Combinations" chart on the butcher paper similar to the chart on page 141. This will be used to collect and discuss group data after groups have completed their practice sheet activities.

Begin this activity by holding a whole-class demonstration. Hold up a half-dollar and present the story from the Teacher Script. Show students how to place coins on the Value Chart Practice Sheet to equal a given value (see sample). Group members will then choose among themselves the values they wish to represent (35 cents, 43 cents, etc.). They write these values in the "Values in Cents" column on page 142. Groups then use page 141 as a manipulative page on which they take turns showing three different coin combinations that equal each chosen value. Each set of coin combinations is then recorded on page 142.

Value Chart Practice Sheet

Directions: Place coins in the columns to show one of the amounts you wrote on page 142. When you are done, complete the information on page 142. Do the same for the other five choices.

Value in Cents	Coins				
	Pennies	Nickels	Dimes	Quarters	Half Dollars
35¢		(coin)	(coin) (coin) (coin)		

When groups have completed the activities, ask students to share the information on page 143 (coin values and coin combinations) with the class. Record their responses on the butcher paper chart. Discuss the results.

Value Charts *(cont.)*

To Simplify: Have an older student or parent volunteer assist each group to talk through the process of completing the chart and practice sheet. Ask the volunteers to review the value of the coins and/or the counting process needed to arrive at the given value.

To Expand: Have students work with values larger than a half-dollar amount. Or, have students write word problems based on the combinations of coins they recorded. They can share these with the class or copy them on task cards for the Math Center. Be sure they make answer keys and give them to you.

Teacher Script: Today you are going to work in your groups to find different ways of showing the same amount of money. *(Hold up a half-dollar.)* How much money do I have in my hand? I am going to give you a problem to solve about this coin. *(Read the following situation to the class.)*

"Megan is at the supermarket. She needs to buy some groceries but she forgot her grocery list. Megan decides to call home to ask her dad about what to buy. But Megan has a problem. She only has a half-dollar in her pocket and she needs change for the public telephone. What change should she ask the clerk for? How many different ways (coin combinations) can you think of to make this same amount (given value of fifty cents)?" (Discuss class responses, noting that they all arrived at the same amount of money but used a variety of coin combinations.)

Let's look at the Value Chart Practice Sheet first. (Discuss the page and demonstrate how to place the appropriate number of coins on the chart to make a given amount. If necessary, model a few coin combinations for the same value.) In your group, choose six money values of fifty cents or less. On page 142, write them in the column labelled "Value in Cents." Then, work together on page 141 to come up with three different ways to show each amount. Write your solutions in the Value Chart Record (page 142).

Now take your math tubs and move into your groups. I will walk around and help.

Evaluation and Processing: Have each group tell about its experiences and discuss the process with the whole class. Ask such questions as these: Did you have any trouble finding three coin combinations for each value? Which coins did you use the most? Which coins did you use the least? Remember to use the anecdotal form on page 18 to keep a record of each student's participation in this activity.

Value Chart Practice Sheet

Directions: Place coins in the columns to show one of the amounts you wrote on page 142. When you are done, complete the information on page 142. Do the same for the other five choices.

Value in Cents	Coins				
	Pennies	Nickels	Dimes	Quarters	Half Dollars

Value Chart Record

Value in Cents

Directions: Write the six coin values you chose in the "Value in Cents" column. Then, write the number of pennies, nickels, dimes, quarters, or half-dollars you combined to make each amount.

Value in Cents	Number of Coins Used				
	Pennies	Nickels	Dimes	Quarters	Half-Dollars

Coin Manipulatives

Math in a Tub Layout

Value Chart Record

Value Chart Practice Sheet

Coins